Hippies

Recent Titles in
Guides to Subcultures and Countercultures

The Ku Klux Klan: A Guide to an American Subculture
Martin Gitlin

Guides to Subcultures and Countercultures

Hippies

A Guide to an American Subculture

Micah L. Issitt

Greenwood Press
An Imprint of ABC-CLIO, LLC

ABC-CLIO

Santa Barbara, California • Denver, Colorado • Oxford, England

Library of Congress Cataloging-in-Publication Data

Issitt, Micah L.
    Hippies : a guide to an American subculture / Micah L. Issitt.
        p. cm.—(Guides to subcultures and countercultures)
    Includes bibliographical references and index.
    ISBN 978-0-313-36572-0 (hard copy : alk. paper)—ISBN 978-0-313-36573-7 (ebook)
  1. Hippies—United States. 2. Subculture—United States. I. Title.
    HQ799.5.I77   2009
    305.5'68—dc22   2009029453

ISBN: 978-0-313-36572-0
EISBN: 978-0-313-36573-7

13   12   11   10   09   1   2   3   4   5

This book is also available on the World Wide Web as an eBook.
Visit www.abc-clio.com for details.

Greenwood Press
An Imprint of ABC-CLIO, LLC

ABC-CLIO, LLC
130 Cremona Drive, P.O. Box 1911
Santa Barbara, California 93116-1911

This book is printed on acid-free paper ∞

Manufactured in the United States of America

To my mother and father,
whom I love more than any hippie ever loved
sex, drugs, or rock & roll.

Contents

Series Foreword

From Beatniks to Flappers, Zoot Suiters to Punks, this series brings to life some of the most compelling countercultures in American history. Designed to offer a quick, in-depth examination and current perspective on each group, the series aims to stimulate the reader's understanding of the richness of the American experience. Each book explores a countercultural group critical to American life and introduces the reader to its historical setting and precedents, the ways in which it was subversive or countercultural, and its significance and legacy in American history. *Webster's Ninth New Collegiate Dictionary* defines counterculture as "a culture with values and mores that run counter to those of established society." Although some of the groups covered can be described as primarily subcultural, they were targeted for inclusion because they have not existed in a vacuum. They have advocated for rules that methodically opposed mainstream culture, or they have lived by their ideals to the degree that it became impossible not to impact the society around them. They have left their marks, both positive and negative, on the fabric of American culture. Volumes cover such groups as Hippies and Beatniks, who impacted popular culture, literature, and art; the Eco-Socialists and Radical

Feminists, who worked toward social and political change; and even groups such as the Ku Klux Klan, who left mostly scars.

A lively alternative to narrow historiography and scholarly monographs, each volume in the *Subcultures and Countercultures* series can be described as a "library in a book," containing both essays and browsable reference materials, including primary documents, to enhance the research process and bring the content alive in a variety of ways. Written for students and general readers, each volume includes engaging illustrations, a timeline of critical events in the subculture, topical essays that illuminate aspects of the subculture, a glossary of subculture terms and slang, biographical sketches of the key players involved, and primary source excerpts—including speeches, writings, articles, first-person accounts, memoirs, diaries, government reports, and court decisions—that offer contemporary perspectives on each group. In addition, each volume includes an extensive bibliography of current recommended print and nonprint sources appropriate for further research.

Preface

What is a hippie? That is one of the primary questions this book will address as we explore the counterculture of the sixties. Though we may accept the dictionary definition of a hippie as a cultural rebel who advocates liberalism in both politics and lifestyle, we will attempt to create a more informed view of the hippies, beyond the list of simple attributes usually ascribed to the group.

The counterculture of the 1960s included a variety of important groups in addition to the hippies, including student activists, civil rights groups like the Black Panthers, and anarchist groups like the Hells Angels motorcycle club. In attempting to simplify the overwhelming complexity of the era, historians often separate the hippies from other groups, but, as we will explore, many of these divisions are largely arbitrary, as each group blended and mixed with the others. I have taken the lingering elements of Beat society as the first embers of hippie culture and a natural point of departure for this exploration.

Though the focus of this history will be counterculture in the United States from 1963 to 1971, the counterculture of the sixties was, in reality, a global phenomenon. Americans, like many cultures around the world, were facing an uncertain future shadowed by the threat of nuclear annihilation. In America and Western Europe, fear of communism developed into a popular panic. The hippie phenomenon in the United States was mirrored by counterculture revolutions in other countries, such as England, Brazil, and France, to name only a few.

Several U.S. neighborhoods became epicenters for the growing counterculture, most notably San Francisco's Haight-Ashbury and New York City's Greenwich Village. This work gives considerable attention to Haight-Ashbury because it was arguably the largest hippie center in the United States; however, it should be acknowledged that the counterculture flourished across the country. The idea that Haight-Ashbury was *the* capital of the hippie craze is not reality, but merely a consequence of the fact that the counterculture in San Francisco, because of its size and activity, garnered the lion's share of the media's attention.

This introduction was developed by examining the literature of the era, provided and created by those who took part in defining the period and by scholars and writers who have examined hippies from a modern perspective. From this material I have prepared a brief historical overview, followed by an exploration of some of the more notable facets of hippie philosophy, culture, and lifestyle. Also included are biographies of renowned hippie-era icons and a collection of interviews and original documents meant to introduce readers to the unique flavor of hippie life.

A full understanding of the hippies cannot be gained solely through scholarly research, but must also include an aesthetic exploration of the music, literature, art, and fashion of the era. The artists mentioned in this book provide an excellent starting point for any reader interested in gaining a more complete understanding of the era. It is my hope that through this work, readers will not only gain a greater appreciation of the historic role of hippie culture, but also of the role that the counterculture plays in creating and manifesting society.

Timeline

1960	First civil rights marches and protests occur in Atlanta.
	Timothy Leary is offered a teaching position at Harvard University.
	Students for a Democratic Society (SDS) holds first meeting in Ann Arbor, Michigan
April 15–17, 1960	The Student Nonviolent Coordinating Committee (SNCC) forms at Shaw University in Raleigh, North Carolina.
May 6, 1960	President Eisenhower signs the Civil Rights Act.
May 11, 1960	Searle receives FDA approval to sell the first birth-control pill, "Enovid," in the United States.
August 9, 1960	Timothy Leary tries psilocybin mushrooms in Cuernavaca, Mexico.

November 4, 1960	John F. Kennedy is elected president of the United States.
1961	President Kennedy creates the Peace Corps.
	Richard Alpert takes psilocybin and joins Leary at Harvard University.
	Peace symbol used in civil rights protest marches by Martin Luther King Jr. and Bayard Rustin.
	Joan Baez and Bob Dylan meet in Greenwich Village.
April 17–19, 1961	Unsuccessful Bay of Pigs Invasion deepens Cold War tensions.
May 1961	Jimi Hendrix enlists in the U.S. Army.
1962	SDS releases the *Port Huron Statement*.
	Bob Dylan releases first album.
	Ken Kesey publishes *One Flew Over the Cuckoo's Nest*.
	The Beatles' "Love, Love Me Do" becomes number 1 hit in the UK.
	Chet Helms, the promoter who will later induct the psychedelic music scene, comes to San Francisco.
	Hugh Romney moves to California.
February 16, 1962	SDS holds antinuclear protest in Washington, DC.
September 1962	Leary and Alpert found International Federation for Internal Freedom (IFIF).
	Rachel Carson's *Silent Spring* is published, ushering in a new era of environmental awareness.
October 1962	Cuban Missile Crisis brings threat of nuclear war to the foreground of the Cold War.

1963	The Battle of Ap Bac in Vietnam is the first major victory of the Viet Cong against the Southern Vietnamese and allied forces.
	LSD first begins to appear as a "street drug," usually sold as liquid drops on cubes of sugar.
	Allen Ginsberg returns to the United States after an extended stay in India where he was introduced to Eastern spirituality.
	Martin Luther King and associates conduct the March on Birmingham, Alabama.
	Janis Joplin arrives in San Francisco with Chet Helms.
June 11, 1963	President Kennedy proposes the Civil Rights Bill.
July 26–28, 1963	Newport Folk Festival features Bob Dylan, Joan Baez, Phil Ochs, and Pete Seeger and gives first hint of the folk, hippie music evolution.
August 28, 1963	Martin Luther King Jr. delivers his "I Have a Dream" speech at the March on Washington.
September 1963	Leary and Alpert are dismissed from Harvard University and move to Millbrook, New York, to continue their experiments with hallucinogens.
November 22, 1963	President Kennedy assassinated in Dallas, Texas.
1964	Ken Kesey and the Merry Pranksters set off for a cross country trip in their "Furthur" bus.
	The Grateful Dead perform first concert together under the name "The Warlocks."
	1090 Page, in Haight-Ashbury, San Francisco, becomes a popular boarding house for traveling hippies and musicians. Janis Joplin and the Grateful Dead stay at the Page house in this year.

	Hugh Romney and his wife found the Hog Farm Collective, one of the nation's most enduring communes.
February 9, 1964	The Beatles appear on *The Ed Sullivan Show* and attract the largest viewing audience in television history.
May 1964	Bob Dylan meets the Beatles on a trip to England and allegedly introduces the Beatles to marijuana.
August 1964	Ken Kesey and the Merry Pranksters visit Timothy Leary and Richard Alpert at Millbrook Estate.
August 28, 1964	Race riots in Philadelphia deepen the civil rights struggle.
December 10, 1964	Martin Luther King is awarded the Nobel Peace Prize.
1965	United States commits first large-scale troop deployment to the conflict in Vietnam, resulting in first mass U.S. protests. The military begins bombing Vietnam on February 8.
	Velvet Underground is formed in New York and performs its first concerts.
	Chet Helms begins promoting concerts for the Family Dog in San Francisco.
	Stanley "Mouse" Miller arrives in San Francisco and he and artist Alton Kelley initiate the psychedelic art scene with promotional posters for the Family Dog.
	First hippie commune, "Drop City," is established on the outskirts of Trinidad, Colorado.
February 21, 1965	Malcolm X assassinated in New York City.
March 1965	Martin Luther King Jr. leads series of demonstrations in Alabama.

April 17, 1965	SDS organizes anti-Vietnam march in Washington, DC, attracting 25,000 supporters. Phil Ochs and Joan Baez perform.
June 1965	Red Dog Saloon, the first psychedelic rock concert hall, opens in Virginia City, Nevada.
September 5, 1965	Journalist Michael Fallon is the first to print the term "hippie" in relation to the youth scene in San Francisco. Term appears in an article about the Blue Unicorn Coffee House.
November 1965	Ken Kesey and Allen Ginsberg organize a "truce" with the Hells Angels and hold first "Acid Test" in La Honda, California.
December 1965	Timothy Leary arrested for possession of marijuana at the Mexico border.
	The Grateful Dead perform first concert under their new name.
1966	The Black Panther Party is formed by Huey P. Newton and Bobby Seale.
	New York disc jockey Bob Fass calls for hippies to gather at LaGuardia Airport for a "Fly-in."
	The Diggers form in San Francisco, under the leadership of Emmett Grogan.
	Chet Helms convinces Janis Joplin to join Big Brother and the Holding Company.
	Jimi Hendrix travels to England and joins with the Experience.
	Grace Slick replaces Signe Anderson as lead singer of Jefferson Airplane and the band performs first concert in San Francisco in November.

January 3, 1966	Ron Thelin opens the Psychedelic Shop in Haight-Ashbury, the country's first "head shop."
January 21–23, 1966	Ken Kesey holds the Trips Festival in San Francisco.
March 11, 1966	Timothy Leary sentenced to 30 years imprisonment for marijuana possession and other charges.
April 7, 1966	Drug company Sandoz restricts medical LSD distribution.
September 1966	Timothy Leary founds his psychedelic church, the League for Spiritual Discovery (LSD).
1967	Jerry Rubin and Abbie Hoffman meet in New York.
	James Taylor is signed by Peter Asher of Apple Records, initiating the singer/songwriter era.
January 14, 1967	The Human Be-In is held in Golden Gate Park; 20,000 fans attend.
February 1967	The United States sends 25,000 troops into Cambodia.
March 26, 1967	New York Be-In held in Central Park attracts 10,000 attendees.
April 1967	Gray Line Bus Company begins taking tourist groups to Haight-Ashbury to view the hippie scene.
June 16–18, 1967	Monterey International Pop Festival introduces a national audience to the underground bands of the Haight-Ashbury. Jimi Hendrix, Janis Joplin, and the Grateful Dead perform.
June 21, 1967	Summer Solstice party in Golden Gate Park sets off the Summer of Love.

August 1967	Rubin and Hoffman drop money on the floor of the New York Stock Exchange.
August 13, 1967	Joan Baez is banned from performing at the Washington Monument after protests from the Daughters of the American Revolution.
October 8, 1967	Che Guevara is killed in Bolivia.
October 10, 1967	The Diggers hold the "Death of the Hippie March" culminating in front of the Psychedelic Shop.
October 21, 1967	Exorcism of the Pentagon, attended by 35,000 demonstrators including Jerry Rubin, Abbie Hoffman, and the Diggers.
1968	The Diggers disband in San Francisco and many leave for communes in rural California.
	Tom Wolfe publishes *The Electric Kool-Aid Acid Test*, based on the activities of Ken Kesey and the Pranksters.
	Timothy Leary publishes *The Politics of Ecstasy*.
January 16, 1968	Rubin and Hoffman officially announce the formation of the Youth International Party (Yippies).
February 1968	The Beatles meet with the Maharishi in India.
April 4, 1968	Martin Luther King Jr. is assassinated in Memphis, Tennessee.
April 23, 1968	SDS representatives take over parts of Columbia University campus.
June 5, 1968	Robert Kennedy is shot in Los Angeles after winning California primary; he dies the next morning.
July 1968	The Nuclear Non-proliferation Treaty is ratified by 61 United Nations member countries.

August 25–26, 1968	Yippies hold Festival of Life (Yip Out) at the Democratic Convention in Chicago. Rubin and Hoffman are two of eight arrested for conspiracy to incite rioting.
December 1968	Joplin leaves Big Brother and the Holding Company to form the Kozmic Blues Band.
April 9, 1969	Beginning of SDS-led demonstrations at Harvard University, which results in members of SDS taking over faculty buildings.
June 1969	The Farm commune is started by Steve Gaskin, formerly head of the Monday Night Class sessions in San Francisco.
July 27, 1969	Police raid in Greenwich Village, results in the Stonewall Uprising in which 2,000 protestors violently clash with police to start the gay rights movement.
August 15–17, 1969	Woodstock Music and Arts Fair becomes the largest hippie gathering in history with over 500,000 attendees.
September 24, 1969	The Chicago Seven trial begins.
October 30, 1969	U.S. Supreme Court orders national desegregation.
November 15, 1969	Largest antiwar rally in U.S. history, with more than 500,000 protestors gathered in Washington, DC.
December 24, 1969	Altamont Concert ends in violence as spectator is killed by Hells Angels security.
1970	Jerry Rubin publishes *Do It: Scenarios of a Revolution*.
January 1, 1970	Nixon signs the National Environmental Policy Act (NEPA) into law.
February 19, 1970	Chicago Seven trial ends; Rubin and Hoffman found guilty of intent to incite rioting.

April 20, 1970	First Earth Day celebrated around the country with an estimated 20 million people taking part in Earth Day events.
September 12, 1970	Timothy Leary escapes prison with assistance from the Weather Underground.
September 18, 1970	Jimi Hendrix dies of drug overdose.
October 4, 1970	Janis Joplin dies of drug overdose.
1971	Richard Alpert publishes classic of hip spirituality *Be Here Now*.
July 3, 1971	Jim Morrison dies in Paris of a drug overdose.
November 1971	Nixon begins withdrawing troops from Vietnam.
December 1971	Greenpeace is founded in Vancouver, Canada.

CHAPTER ONE

Historical
Overview

From Beats to Hippies

There is no simple answer to the question "Where does the counter-culture come from?" The development of any cultural group is the result of numerous influences converging within the framework of the broader environment. The simplest explanation is that counterculture emerges in *reaction* to facets of mainstream culture. The hippies emerged from the mainstream culture of the 1950s and 1960s, follow-ing in the footsteps of an earlier counterculture group, the rebellious youth movement known as the Beat Generation.

The Beats and hippies both emerged from what writer Mark Lytle called the "Era of Consensus." In the 1950s, as Cold War hysteria swept across America, the social environment became increasingly con-servative and repressive, including government censorship of literature, speech, and other forms of expression. In addition, there was a rise in "consumerism" in America, a complex social phenomenon marked by a popular obsession with material gain. These and other related factors gave rise to a rebellious youth movement known as the Beat Genera-tion, a group that the popular media later called "Beatniks."[1]

Hippies greet each other in Golden Gate Park. (© 2009 Robert Altman. Used by permission. Appears in Robert Altman, The Sixties *[Santa Monica Press, 2007].)*

The leaders of the Beat movement were primarily young intellectuals who set themselves apart from the mainstream by their lifestyle choices, including the types of clothing they wore, the music they listened to, and how they approached relationships, employment, and politics. The music of the movement was jazz and "revival" folk, quintessentially represented by artists like Woody Guthrie, whose songs were part protest, part soul-searching commentary.[2]

At the core of Beat culture were still-notable poets and literary figures like Jack Kerouac and Allen Ginsberg, both of whom helped to build one of the first centers of Beat culture, in North Beach, San Francisco, and helped to spread the culture around the country.[3] The Beat movement spread across the country through the jazz and coffeehouse scenes. Soon, every city had clubs where local Beats would gather to discuss literature, politics, and other intellectual pursuits. In *The Beat Generation in San Francisco*, writer Lawrence Ferlinghetti describes the Beats as "Stone Age Hippies," noting that many of the things that fascinated the Beats—Eastern religion, pacifism, ecological consciousness, homosexual rights, and hedonistic lifestyles—became hallmarks of hippie culture as well.[4]

In a pattern that would repeat with the hippies in the late 1960s, Beat culture grew so popular in the late 1950s that it became a caricature of its original ideals. Thousands of fad seekers flocked to New York and San Francisco, calling themselves "Beatniks," and as a result the original Beats abandoned their scene. As writer William Burroughs muses, "Ginsberg opened a million coffee bars and sold a million pairs of Levi's to both sexes. Woodstock rises from his pages."[5]

The Hippies Emerge: 1960–1965

The political environment of 1960 America informed and inspired many teenaged Americans to join the hippie rebellion. The civil rights movement was gaining steam, America had officially sent thousands of troops to Vietnam, and the antinuclear movement was building in response to ongoing Cold War tensions. The cultural environment was also changing. Beat literature had found its way to colleges and universities and was influencing a new generation of students. Disc jockeys around the country were furthering the racial integration of popular culture by introducing white audiences to "race music," and the folk revival of the late 1950s was blending into the doo-wop rock of the early 1960s.[6]

While the hippie vibe was developing around the country, there were several areas—most notably Haight-Ashbury in San Francisco, Greenwich Village in New York, and the Sunset Strip in Los Angeles—which, because of their location, history, and population, were uniquely suited to become the major epicenters of sixties counterculture. The main hippie areas began as blue-collar communities with one common factor: affordable housing. Cheap housing attracted a diverse population and, in the 1950s, most of what would become the hippie neighborhoods had mixed populations of African Americans, whites, Hispanics, and gays and lesbians living in relative harmony. The ethnic and cultural diversity of these neighborhoods fostered a socially progressive environment, as only those who were comfortable with alternative lifestyles chose to live there.

The Beats were the first counterculture group to settle in Greenwich Village and established their own alternative businesses there, including coffeehouses, bookstores, and music stores that catered to the new trends rather than mainstream tastes. The transformation of the Village from Beat to hippie occurred gradually from the late 1950s to the mid-1960s. In San Francisco the former Beats and the newly arriving hippies gradually migrated from North Beach to the Haight-Ashbury neighborhood beginning in the early 1960s. In other cities around the country, the hippies moved into and eventually took over many of the neighborhoods and establishments that formerly catered to the Beats.

While many of the older residents in neighborhoods like the Haight-Ashbury and Greenwich Village resented the arrival of their new, bohemian neighbors, most felt obligated to try to accept the new arrivals. It was precisely because the neighborhoods were progressive that they were vulnerable to the counterculture invasion. By the end of the 1960s, many of these progressive neighborhoods had been completely transformed into urban hippie utopias, where hippies outnumbered the original residents.

The early sixties also saw the beginning of the psychedelic movement, driven by two "gurus" who made it their mission to introduce a generation of youth to the potential of the psychedelic experience. On the West Coast was Ken Kesey, a former Beat writer who would later tour the country on his "Furthur" bus, and who introduced thousands of young hippies to their first psychedelic experiences. On the East Coast in 1962 Timothy Leary and his colleagues began studying the scientific side of hallucinogens at Harvard University, and they later became the major proponents of "psychedelic spirituality."[7]

While Leary and Kesey were both important to the developing counterculture attitudes on drug use, Leary's scholarly psychedelic spirituality and Kesey's hallucinogen-fueled dance parties were at opposite ends of the spectrum. In 1964 Kesey and friends visited Leary at his compound in Millbrook, New York, and although the two did not see eye to eye, the event was recorded in hippie lore as a historic meeting of the gurus.[8]

Just before mid-decade, another major event helped to set the stage for the rise of the hippies—the British Invasion. It was in 1964 that American audiences first heard the Beatles and the Rolling Stones, two groups who would play major roles in the development of the hippie music scene. The new sound from England blended rock, blues, folk, and doo-wop in ways not yet imagined by American bands, and the result was explosive, setting off a sonic revolution.[9]

The Height and the Haight

By most accounts, 1965 was the year that the hippies took over. It was during this year that many of the quintessential "hippie bands" were formed or became popular, including the Doors, the Grateful Dead, and the Velvet Underground. In addition, hundreds of underground bands emerged in cities across the country, many imitating the new sound from London.

Before 1965, hippie culture was still in an inchoate state, arising from the ashes of Beat culture with an influx of Carnaby Street mod and Greenwich Village folk revival. After 1965 there would be no doubt, at least to the mainstream media and the millions who tuned in to it, that San Francisco was at the center of this strange new cultural phenomena.

In Haight-Ashbury, called "Hashbury" by the hippies, some of the new residents set up "flophouses," where travelers and touring bands could stay for a few nights. The boarding houses at 1090 Page Street and 1836 Pine Street became the most famous because of the celebrities who later stayed there, including Janis Joplin and the Grateful Dead. The Pine and Page flophouses were also impromptu concert halls, where a host of underground Bay Area bands performed before moving on to the larger venues like the Avalon Ballroom or the Fillmore West.

The psychedelic rock scene began in the basements of the Haight's boarding houses but came into its own in Virginia City, Nevada, where a group of San Francisco hippies established the Red Dog Saloon. The Red Dog was a concert hall, operated by a San Francisco psychedelic band known as the Charlatans and designed to look like the saloon from the popular television western *Gunsmoke*. In the summer of 1965, Virginia City was transformed into a hippie paradise. Hundreds flocked to the Red Dog that summer, many wearing

The Jefferson Airplane plays the Family Dog by the Bay, 1969. (© 2009 Robert Altman. Used by permission. Appears in Robert Altman, The Sixties *[Santa Monica Press, 2007].)*

old western or Victorian-style clothing, elements of what became known as "hippie high costume."[10]

The Red Dog closed down after a single summer, and the Charlatans returned to San Francisco. That same year, a group of hippies who operated the flophouse on Pine Street and had spent the summer in Virginia City formed the "Family Dog" in the Haight, a communal organization that held psychedelic concerts, conferences on Eastern spirituality, and a variety of other hippie-flavored events. Among them were promoter Chet Helms, and Luria Castell, a former student activist who became a major player in the early Haight scene. The Family Dog also hired graphic artists like Alton Kelley, whose unique artistic style became emblematic of hippie culture in general.

Kesey and his psychedelic touring group, called the "Merry Pranksters," were also in San Francisco as the Haight scene began to capture national attention. Kesey and his long-time colleague Ken Babbs began holding "acid tests," parties in which guests were given

LSD in an effort to "test" their spiritual and mental state. The first acid test was held in November of 1965, followed by a second in December. The largest of Kesey's acid parties was the January 1966 Trips Festival at the Haight's Longshoremen's Hall, where several hundred gathered for music, dancing, and revelry. The acid tests in part inspired the large hippie gatherings of 1967 and the outdoor concert craze, as many Bay Area bands cut their teeth at Kesey's hallucinogen-fueled parties.[11]

While many in the Haight came for the parties, some in the community were dedicated to the idea of fomenting cultural revolution. The Diggers, a political/social outreach group that formed in 1966, were the most recognizable symbol of hippie politics. Most of the Diggers had previously been members of the San Francisco Mime Troupe, an urban theater organization known for its provocative political plays. The Diggers' goal was to inspire the members of this "new cultural community" to become true revolutionaries.

The Diggers eschewed traditional models of morality and legality and believed that, if the Haight community worked together, they could create a society free from consumerism, where food and other goods were given free or in return for other services. Toward this end, the Diggers passed out free food to panhandling hippies in an area of Golden Gate Park known, ironically, as the panhandle. The Diggers also set up a free store where members of the community could get free food and other goods. What the Diggers couldn't obtain legally, they stole from area merchants. This banditry, coupled with the Diggers' seeming delight at confronting the police, put them at odds with the law. The Diggers never reached their ultimate goals, finding that most hippies were far more interested in having fun than participating in a social revolution. By the late 1960s, the Diggers, who were leaders to the first wave of hippies, were as critical of the new hippie scene as they were of mainstream culture.[12]

As more and more hippies began coming to the Haight, the existing residents became concerned they were losing control of their neighborhood. When the Haight Street Merchants Organization refused to admit many of the new, hip businesses into their ranks, Ron Thelin, a local merchant and member of the hippie community, organized an alternative merchant's group, called the Haight Independent Proprietors (HIP) organization.

Thelin opened the Psychedelic Shop, San Francisco's first "head shop," at 1535 Haight Street in 1966. Thelin's goal was to create a link between the hippie community and the mainstream community, and to help ease tensions between the two groups. The HIP merchants attended public meetings, met with police, and helped organize community events and services. Many posted signs in their windows with pictures of the undercover cops in the neighborhood in an effort to help hippies avoid the law, and some passed out whistles so that those threatened by the police could call for help.

It was around this time that Herb Caen, a columnist for the *San Francisco Chronicle*, began using the term "hippie" in his columns, primarily to refer to members of the HIP merchants rather than the kids on the street.[13] It was writer Michael Fallon who first called the San Francisco kids "hippies" in a 1965 article called "A New Haven for Beatniks" published about the Blue Unicorn Coffee House, where members of the early "legalize marijuana" movement would meet. By 1967, the mainstream media latched onto the terminology and the kids on the San Francisco streets would forever be known as the "hippies."[14]

Let's Come Together

While hippie culture was gaining steam in San Francisco, New York's Lower East Side, which had been a major Mecca for the Beat Generation, already had a thriving hippie scene of its own. Though the media ultimately spent more time and ink on the ostentatious San Francisco scene, New York had hippie kids by the thousands and areas like Greenwich Village were alive with communal apartments,

Head Shops

Recreational drugs, a major part of the hip lifestyle, spawned a cottage industry based on selling smoking equipment to marijuana users and psychedelic aids to hallucinogen fans. The origin of the name "head shop" is uncertain, but avid marijuana smokers were, and still are, called "pot heads."

recreational drugs, and gurus preaching to packed houses of students and spiritual seekers.

The New York scene was more driven by intellectual activism than was the West Coast scene, and the bands from New York were quite different. The Velvet Underground, headlined by Lou Reed, was one of the most lasting sixties bands to emerge from New York, but Reed and his fellow band members never considered themselves hippies. In sharp contrast to the upbeat twanging of Haight Street's hippies, the Velvet Underground's songs were comparatively dismal. Among other topics, Reed wrote songs about gender reassignment surgery, heroin addiction, and homosexual prejudice.[15]

The growth of the hippie culture was in large part due to the continued work of radio DJs and the alternative press. New York City's Bob Fass, who headlined the famous *Radio Unnameable* program on WBAI, put out a call in late 1966 for hippies across the city to get together for a "Fly In" at LaGuardia International Airport.[16] While hippies had been gathering by the hundreds for parties like the 1966 Trips Festival, thanks to Fass and others like him, hippies began gathering by the thousands.

The now infamous Gathering of the Tribes (a/k/a the Human Be-In), held in San Francisco's Golden Gate Park on January 14, 1967, made national news and attracted as many as 20,000 hippies from across the country. This was the story the media had been waiting for—an event of sufficient proportions that they could bring this new scene to the public's attention. Those looking to condemn the hippies showed pictures of scantily clad women and told stories of unbridled indecency, drug use, and immorality. Those who wanted to celebrate the scene showed pictures and told stories of the biggest hippie party the world had ever seen. Thousands of hippies made the trek to San Francisco, where they were told there were more parties happening all the time.

Some of the more industrious members of the scene began dreaming of ways to capitalize on the potential revenues from the new population. The result was the 1967 Monterey International Pop Festival, the first of the big outdoor music concerts, which marked the moment when Haight's garage bands hit the national scene. Monterey Pop was the precipitating event that led to the now-famous "Summer of Love," when upwards of 100,000 hippies from around

---

Coast to Coast

As hundreds of hippies made the trek from East Coast to West, many drove along portions of the path laid out for the Lincoln Highway, the world's first transcontinental highway. The 3,389-mile Lincoln was second only to Route 66 in the pantheon of America's famous roads.

---

the country came to San Francisco, the place that the media crowned the "hippie kingdom."[17]

For many hippies, the Summer of Love was the beginning of the end. The influx of kids to Haight-Ashbury made the neighborhood intolerable to many of the original residents. The sheer number of hippies created a host of problems. Drug abuse and homelessness were common, young hippies were subjected to violence, and dozens of young women were raped. In response, the Diggers and the Family Dog joined forces with local merchants and *The Oracle*, the most prominent of the alternative press newspapers in the area, to form the Council for the Summer of Love, in an effort to prepare for and deal with the arrival of so many new residents.[18]

San Francisco and parts of Monterey had become caricatures of hippie culture. In Haight-Ashbury, a tour company offered bus tours of the hippie hangouts and hundreds of new stores opened up to sell "hippie" clothing, music, and other paraphernalia. In October of 1967, dismayed by the commercialization of their culture, the Diggers held a "Death of the Hippie March," coinciding with Ron Thelin's decision to close his Psychedelic Shop, one of the first hippie businesses on Haight Street. The march culminated in a gathering in front of Thelin's shop, where the assembled crowd buried the Psychedelic Shop's sign. For the Diggers and others gathered that day, it was a symbolic end to the golden age of the hippies, which had only lasted for a few short years.[19]

Increased publicity also brought increased attention from the police and other government agencies. Pressure began mounting from outside, and hippies found it increasingly hard to find housing, employment, or any of the other amenities of residency. By early

1968, the Diggers disbanded and many of the hippie luminaries fled the neighborhood, moving to other parts of San Francisco or to other cities.

The San Francisco Be-In and the Summer of Love were followed by similar action on the East Coast. In 1968 a group of hippies led by Jerry Rubin and his Youth International Party ("Yippies"), staged the Easter Sunday Be-In in Central Park's Sheep's Head Meadow. The Easter Be-In, which Rubin and followers called a "Yip-Out," attracted nearly 30,000 gatherers and, for the Yippies, served as a perfect venue to spread their political message.[20]

Rubin, Abbie Hoffman, and their friends blended revolutionary politics with lighthearted pranks, representing a true middle ground between the hippies and the more serious student activist movement. Even before the Yip-Out, Rubin and the Yippies had been staging high-profile events, including gathering thousands of hippies in Washington, DC, in 1967, in an attempt to "levitate the Pentagon." The crowd was later estimated at over 50,000.[21]

The culmination of the Yippies' activities was the Democratic Convention of 1968 where they staged a massive party, called the "Youth Festival" or the "Festival of Life," which was intended to be part protest, part Be-In. The Chicago police were not willing to allow the Yippies to disrupt the convention and violence ensued. In the aftermath, Rubin, Hoffman, and six others were arrested and charged with conspiracy to incite rioting and other related crimes.

The resulting trial lasted almost a year and included a "who's who" of hippie-era celebrities testifying on behalf of the men who came to be known as the "Chicago Seven." Among those who spoke out for the accused were Allen Ginsberg, Timothy Leary, and folksingers Judy Collins and Pete Seeger.[22]

The lasting importance of the Chicago Seven trial was that it brought the hippie rebellion into direct conflict with its primary enemy—the political system at large. "The case raised profound issues concerning the scope of conspiracy law in the context of confrontational political demonstrations," wrote Alan Dershowitz in *America on Trial*.[23] Beyond the legal ramifications, the trial of the Chicago Seven was *the* hippie political event of the era. Political activist and Chicago Seven member Tom Hayden called the trial "a watershed experience for a whole generation of alienated white youth."[24]

The Highs and Lows

While some say "true hippieism" died in 1967, the kids who came to San Francisco that summer saw a scene very much alive. For them, hippie culture was at its peak and it was time to revel in the camaraderie, the bohemian ethos, and the music. The Monterey concert brought hippie music into the mainstream, and performers like Janis Joplin, the Doors, and Jimi Hendrix were now at the tops of the pop charts.

The Woodstock Music and Art Fair of 1969 was a major moment in the history of American rock music. Despite a host of technical and logistical issues, the concert captured the imagination of a generation and has become a symbol of hippie culture and a badge of honor for those who were there. As described by Andy Bennett in *Remembering Woodstock*, "Woodstock has acquired legendary status as both the *defining* and the *last great moment* of the 1960s, a decade which saw large scale social upheavals and significant cultural transformations."[25]

In December of 1969, four months after Woodstock, came the Altamont Free Concert at California's Altamont Speedway. The Rolling Stones, who had not been able to perform at Woodstock, were the headlining act. In what would come to be seen as a major blunder on the part of organizers, the Hells Angels were hired for security. As the crowd became heated after hours of delays waiting for the Stones to take the stage, a fight erupted near the stage. When a young African American man pulled a gun, he was knifed to death by several Angels.[26]

The relationship between the Angels and the hippies had always been taut. At times they could see eye to eye, as both groups were outside the mainstream and shared a sense of being cultural outlaws. In 1965 Ken Kesey arranged a party with his Pranksters and numerous other hippie icons to meet with members of the Hells Angels. The party became a bridge between the two groups, as Kesey convinced the Angels to allow peace marches and other antiwar protests, which they had previously disrupted in the name of patriotism.[27]

At Altamont the Hells Angels and the hippies realized that they weren't kindred spirits, but forces at opposite ends of the spectrum of rebellion. Bill Thompson, former manager for Jefferson Airplane, said of the concert, "Altamont was the end of the sixties. It was December 1969, and that was the end. Of the whole feeling. We kept on going but it was a different feeling."[28]

If 1969 was a major blow to the hippie vibe, 1970 took a toll on hippie music. Janis Joplin and Jimi Hendrix died that year, followed by Jim Morrison in 1971. The deaths of these musical giants, stars of psychedelic rock and symbols of the West Coast scene, were also symbolic of the ways in which drug culture was beginning to change. While hard drugs like heroin and cocaine had long been part of the drug scene, these drugs were now flowing through areas like the Haight-Ashbury, and many of the more idealistic hippies fled the scene to avoid the violence and "bad vibes." "The kids went out to the country," said writer Michael Stepanian, "Bolinas, Santa Rosa, Healdsburg, Auburn, Santa Cruz. Basically, they all left the city and it became a very different situation."[29] As hard drugs replaced dope and many of the more dedicated hippies left to pursue their ideals in other areas, hippie-ism, as it had been, was dead.

In 1976 writer Tom Wolfe labeled the 1970s the " 'Me' decade," a criticism of the self-absorbed, trend-obsessed nature of pop culture in that era. Ideas that the hippies brought to popular attention, like Yoga and Eastern philosophy, became trends in the 1970s, along with a wave of other obsessions like Silva Mind Control, health food, and jogging. Historian Christopher Lasch summarized the evolution of American culture, saying that a "lust for immediate gratification pervades American society from top to bottom."[30]

Most historians and former hippies agree that the hippie "thing" ended in the early to mid-1970s. It is perhaps incorrect to say that the hippies "died"; more accurately, the underlying themes and

---

Vibes

Hippies believed it was possible to detect positive or negative energy, called "vibes," from a person, place, or thing. Positive energy was to be sought out while negative energy was to be avoided. More than mere slang, vibes symbolized the belief that reliable information could be gained by attending to one's innate feelings about the world.

inspirations that fueled the hippies were absorbed into popular culture, rendering their counterculture function obsolete. The peace sign, once a serious symbol of political rebellion, became a popular decorative pattern. Yoga and meditation, once seen as earnest attempts to achieve new levels of spiritual consciousness, became fitness fads, and Buddhism, once a potent rejection of Judeo-Christian dominance in America, became a vehicle for self-help literature.

Some former hippies, still dedicated to the underlying ideals of the movement, continued to pursue that lifestyle in new ways. Communes remained, though they moved to outlying, rural communities. Perhaps most important, hippies taught their children to see the world in a different light. By the 21st century, many of the ideas that hippies thought of as "revolutionary" were common sense for a generation fueled by what the hippies had accomplished. While the hippie era was short-lived, its effect was profound. The cultural revolution envisioned by the hippies was realized not immediately, but gradually, trickling through generations and pervasively chipping away at the status quo.

Hippie Life

Who were the hippies?

In trying to answer this question, it is important to recognize that there were two basic tiers to hippie culture: leaders and followers. It is perhaps easiest to view the hippie era as a phenomenon brought about by a small number of cultural leaders—philosophers, writers, musicians, activists, and politicians—and the thousands of young people, in America and across the world, who were inspired by them.

While the leaders are well known, the youth who constituted the substrate of hippie culture are all too often grouped into a stereotypical mold, created by those who found themselves in a position to judge and study the hippies, whether to condemn or celebrate them. There never was a "standard hippie," whose behavior or beliefs could accurately represent the counterculture. Rather, hippies were a group made up of thousands of individuals, engaged in a multitude of activities, whose presence in and effect on society has been abbreviated in the necessity for historical simplification.

The hippie lifestyle, as it was lived on the streets of any city in the United States, can be investigated by examining the ways that hippies approached their lives, notably those lifestyle choices for which the hippies became famous: sexuality, recreational drug use, music culture, and involvement in the political movements that defined the period.

The Liberal Rebellion

The central tenant of hippie philosophy, as stated by Timothy Miller in *The Hippies and American Values*, is "If it feels good, then do it so long as it doesn't hurt anyone else."[31] When deconstructed, this "creed" has two components: first, it is good to live a hedonist lifestyle, and second, in an ideal society there will be no rules governing consensual behavior. In other words, the hippies believed in doing things that feel good and, so long as no one gets hurt, everyone should be free to engage in any activity deemed pleasurable or positive.[32]

This general philosophy was implicitly accepted by the hippies and governed the way they lived their daily lives. Hippies sought out pleasure, encouraged others to seek pleasure, and rebelled against any social convention, law, or tradition seen as an attempt to curtail "natural" impulses and desires. Hippies also celebrated any tradition, philosophy, or activity (e.g., drugs, sex, music) that had the potential to heighten the pleasurable experience of life.

To understand the hippie focus on pleasure and hedonism, it is necessary to understand the culture from which the hippies emerged. A variety of social and cultural factors converged in the 1940s and 1950s to create what has been called a culture of "consensus."[33] Whether this was a "real" quality of the environment or simply an expression of angst among the younger generation, the hippies felt that society was dominated by conservative values and materialism.

According to writer and historian Mark Lytle, the Beats were the first counterculture group that "subjected the Cold War consensus and social conformity to a penetrating critique."[34] The hippies found heroes among the Beats and followed in their footsteps, becoming the next generation of critics to question the status quo in American culture. The hippies saw materialism, militant politics, and social repression as the ills of society, and they rebelled largely by living outside the expectations and the accepted norms of mainstream culture.

Hippie rebellion against the mainstream took many forms, but one of the primary modes of fighting the system was to emphasize "individualism" and "hedonism" as guiding goals in the hip life. This focus was a direct rejection of the "consensus" of the previous period, which emphasized putting one's own pleasure second to the stability of family and society. In sharp contrast, the hippies said "me first" and boldly declared that they would live pleasurable lives, even if mainstream society said it was wrong or illegal.

From a philosophical perspective, the hippies' emphasis on individual rights and freedoms places them in the school known as "classical liberalism," which was pioneered by Western philosophers like John Locke and Adam Smith. Like the liberalists, the hippies believed that the peaceful pursuit of one's own happiness, coupled with the willingness to cooperate for mutual goals, was the recipe for an ideal society. Unlike the intellectual reasoning of Locke and Smith, hippie liberalism was chaotic and largely based on rejecting mainstream (often conservative) political/social philosophy, which was blamed for the lamentable state of American culture.[35]

In the 21st century, contemporary liberals often focus on equal opportunity and access to material goods; however, the defense of personal liberty remains an important part of the liberal worldview. Long after the hippie scene dissipated, the idea of the "hippie" is still inextricably tied, in the popular imagination, to liberalism and individual rights.

It is inaccurate to assume that most hippies saw themselves as activists or part of a social movement. Many hippies, for their part, did little more than conform to the rules and trends created within

The Kids Are Alright

To mainstream America, the hippie philosophy seemed childish, and this was reflected in the words used to describe them, like "flower children." While hippies took themselves seriously, they also accepted the distinction that they were the young generation, often using terms denoting maturity to describe their opponents, like "the man."

the counterculture. However, the hippie lifestyle itself was a form of rebellion, defined by defiance of cultural norms, emphasis on personal fulfillment, and acceptance of diversity as the model of a more enjoyable, more equitable society.

Notes

1. Mark Lytle, *America's Uncivil Wars: The Sixties Era from Elvis to the Fall of Richard Nixon* (New York: Oxford University Press, 2006), 7–10.
2. John Patrick Diggins, *The Proud Decades: America in War and in Peace, 1941–1960* (New York: W. W. Norton, 1989), 265–80.
3. Michael Davidson, *The San Francisco Renaissance* (New York: Cambridge University Press, 1991), 30–40.
4. Bill Morgan, *The Beat Generation in San Francisco: A Literary Tour* (San Francisco: City Lights Books, 2003), xiii–xiv.
5. Matt Theado, *The Beats: A Literary Reference* (New York: Carroll Y. Graf Publishers, 2003), 117.
6. Jean-Christophe Agnew and Roy Rosenzweig, *A Companion to Post-1945 America* (Boston: Blackwell, 2002), 328–36.
7. Timothy Leary, *High Priest*, 2nd ed. (San Francisco: Ronin Publishing, 1995), 11, 157.
8. Barry Miles, *Hippie* (New York: Sterling Publishing, 2004), 34.
9. Bill Harry, *The British Invasion: How the Beatles and Other UK Bands Conquered America* (London: Chrome Dreams, 2004).
10. Alice Echols, *Shaky Ground: The '60s and Its Aftershocks* (New York: Columbia University Press, 2002), 35–40.
11. Mick Sinclair and John-Henri Holmberg, *San Francisco: A Cultural and Literary History* (Berkeley: Signal Books, 1995), 199–202.
12. Martin Torgoff, *Can't Find My Way Home: America in the Great Stoned Age, 1945–2000* (New York: Simon and Schuster, 2004), 200–205.
13. Dominick Cavallo, *A Fiction of the Past: The Sixties in American History* (New York: Macmillan, 2001), 116–19.
14. Michael Fallon, "A New Paradise for Beatniks," *San Francisco Examiner*, September 5, 1965, 5.
15. Joe Harvard, *The Velvet Underground and Nico* (New York: Continuum, 2004), 21–50.
16. Jeff Land, *Active Radio: Pacifica's Brash Experiment* (Minneapolis: University of Minnesota Press, 1999), 134–40.
17. Martin A. Lee and Bruce Shlain, *Acid Dreams: The CIA, LSD, and the Sixties Rebellion* (New York: Grove Press, 1985), 193–96.
18. Echols, *Shaky Ground*, 43–45.

19. Lisa Montanarelli and Ann Harrison, *Strange but True San Francisco: Tales of the City by the Bay* (Guilford, CT: Globe Pequot Press, 2005), 210.
20. David Farber, *Chicago '68* (Chicago: University of Chicago Press, 1994), 37.
21. Jeffrey W. Fenn, *Levitating the Pentagon: Evolutions in the American Theatre of the Vietnam War Era* (Newark: University of Delaware Press, 1992), 20–22.
22. John Campbell McMillian and Paul Buhle, eds., *The New Left Revisited*, Critical Perspectives on the Past (Philadelphia: Temple University Press, 2003), 200.
23. Alan M. Dershowitz, *America on Trial: Inside the Legal Battles That Transformed Our Nation* (Clayton, Australia: Warner Books, 2004), 393.
24. John Downton Hazlett, *My Generation: Collective Autobiography and Identity Politics* (Madison: University of Wisconsin Press, 1998), 68–70.
25. Andy Bennett, *Remembering Woodstock* (Surrey: Ashgate Publishing, Ltd., 2004), xiv.
26. Douglas B. Holt, *How Brands Become Icons: The Principles of Cultural Branding* (Cambridge, MA: Harvard Business Press, 2004), 165–66.
27. Lee and Shlain, *Acid Dreams*, 125–26.
28. Bill Graham and Robert Greenfield, *Bill Graham Presents: My Life Inside Rock and Out* (New York: Da Capo Press, 2004), 297.
29. Ibid., 196.
30. James T. Patterson, *Restless Giant: The United States from Watergate to Bush v. Gore* (New York: Oxford University Press, 2005), 68–71.
31. Timothy Miller, *The Hippies and American Values* (Knoxville: University of Tennessee Press, 1991), 29.
32. Preston Shires, *Hippies of the Religious Right: From the Counterculture of Jerry Garcia to the Subculture of Jerry Falwell* (Waco, TX: Baylor University Press, 2007), 24–26.
33. Lytle, *America's Uncivil Wars*, 4–10.
34. Ibid., 7.
35. Robert Higgs, et al., *The Challenge of Liberty* (Washington, DC: The Independent Institute, 2006), 1–50.

CHAPTER TWO | Sex and the Hip Body

When viewed from the 21st century, American attitudes about sex in the early 1960s were highly conservative. Few Americans spoke openly about sexuality and, while the pleasurable nature of sex was widely acknowledged; nudity, sexual contact, and sexual discourse were viewed as "private" activities. The very idea that something as inherently pleasurable as sex, which is not only the basis of reproduction but also of the formation of family bonds, should be considered "indecent" or "secretive" was anathema to the hippies and their obsession with liberty, self expression, and the pursuit of pleasure.

In true rebellious fashion, the hippies brought sex from the bedroom to the living room and challenged America to watch. Hip sex had two basic factors: rebellion and love. Within the culture, sexuality was cast in a new light as the hippies aggressively rebelled against the "dirty" or "shameful" view of sex, while promoting sex as the ultimate expression of unity, compassion, and love. For the hippies, sex was something to be celebrated rather than hidden, encouraged rather than scorned.

While they did not always explicitly support alternative sexuality, the hippies helped prepare society to tackle issues like homosexuality, body image, and feminism. The 1960s also mark the period within the larger "sexual revolution" when Americans became more

---

Woodstock Babies

Legend holds that two babies were born at the 1969 Woodstock Concert. Considering that most hippie women felt that concert attendance while 8+ months pregnant was "far out," the claim seemed plausible. While there was undeniably enough sex going on to conceive thousands of children, investigations failed to find the alleged progeny.

---

comfortable with the idea that young women could have sex outside of marriage and for pleasure.[1] These and other aspects of hip sexuality helped to bring about major changes in cultural stereotypes and formed an essential component of the basic hippie lifestyle.

Free Love

The term "free love" is sometimes used to describe the hippie sexual ideal. The phrase was meant to convey both the idea that sex should be conducted in an environment and spirit of love, and the idea that people should be free to have sex with whomever they choose, without reference to the rules and morals of mainstream society.

Theologian and activist John Humphrey Noyes coined the term "free love" in 1848 when he formed the Oneida Community, a religious cult that practiced "group marriage." Within the Oneida Community, individuals were married to and expected to have sex with all group members of the opposite sex, which Noyes believed would discourage the formation of "special" relationships, possessiveness, and sexual jealousy. Noyes saw these factors as primary agents in the disintegration of community.

Some hippies shared the belief that possessiveness and jealousy were negative emotional states, and that an enlightened person could engage in sex openly without the need to possess his or her lover.[2] However, the hippies might also have criticized Noyes for substituting one set of rules for another when the ultimate ideal, to the hippies, was to love openly, without rules. To them, the goal in rejecting mainstream society's sexual standards was to free individuals to "do their own thing."

To the hippies, exclusive relationships were not inherently negative; rather it was society's view that *only* exclusive relationships were
acceptable that needed to be challenged. Toward this end, many hippies also rejected the idea of "fidelity" in marriage. Some hippies pur-
sued extramarital affairs, sometimes with the consent of their spouses,
and many hippies engaged in short terms affairs with multiple part-
ners. Some adventurous hippies engaged in "swinging" and group sex,
though this was still not the norm in hippie culture.[3] Though some
chose an alternative path, most hippies engaged in exclusive relationships and many eventually married.

The primary focus of the free love movement was to abandon the
idea that sex before or outside of marriage was "dirty" and/or "sinful,"
and to advocate a "new morality," in which sex for pleasure was no less
important than sex for reproduction. In the words of sociologist and
professor Gordon Clanton, in a 1969 article published in *Christian
Century*, "We must begin to teach that sex is morally neutral. Properly
understood and lovingly practiced, sex outside of marriage is indeed a
positive good."[4]

By treating sex as just another form of pleasure, like eating, sleeping, or playing, the hippies hoped to free themselves from the sexual
obsession of the masses, in which sex was often used to control behavior. As writer David Allyn put it in *Make Love, Not War*, "For hippies,
sexual liberation meant not being preoccupied with sex." The hippies
substituted a sexual ethos that mirrored their basic philosophy, in
which sex was based on pleasure, free choice, and most important,
love. The phrase "Make love, not war" was, in Allyn's analysis, not a
plea for sexual contact but rather for "making love," which is defined
as the most profound contact between individuals, including but not
limited to sexual contact. "Love was the central tenant of the counterculture," wrote Allyn, "love of nature, love of life, love of oneself, love
of love. Sexual intercourse was merely a way to communicate with,
and express love for, another person."[5]

Nudity

Another major facet of hip sexuality was the acceptance of nudity, a
crucial step toward addressing the issues of "body image" in American

culture. Hippies reveled in the simple pleasure of being nude, both in public and in private, which contrasted sharply with mainstream attitudes about nudity. Though nudist communities existed before the hippies, hip nudists challenged societal norms by flaunting their nudity in public, despite objections and laws prohibiting "indecency."

Hippie views on nudity ranged from playful to profound. In a 1968 issue of the newspaper *Matrix*, one hippie wrote, "When the genitals lose their special significance then people will cease to fear them and so cease to need to build special monuments to them. It is because they are hidden that they are ugly and dirty."[6] In contrast, many hippies simply realized that it was fun to be nude. The fact that nudity was shocking to some "straights" made it all the more fun.

Nudity in the hippie era was profoundly different than the display of nudity in previous eras or in the decades since. Nude magazines like *Playboy*, which predated hippies, portrayed nudity in a stylized and highly strategic manner, wherein sexual images were (and still are) used to market products. While the hippies didn't abandon the consumer aspect of nudity, they inspired a new aesthetic that envisioned the raw human body as an object of beauty. Consumer culture was informed by this view and soon models in magazines were wearing less makeup and were often pictured in naturalistic surroundings.

In *Nudity: A Cultural Anatomy*, writer Ruth Barcan argues "For the hippies, nudity served as both a symbol of and a pathway to social and sexual liberation."[7] The revolutionary nature of nudity was certainly not taken for granted by the hippies who sometimes used nudity as a form of protest against, among other things, prevalent attitudes about decency. Perhaps the hippies' greatest contribution to

---

Hippie High Costume

From peace signs to body paint, hippie fashion was a decoupage of style, self-expression, and rebellion. At the "red carpets" of hip society, hippies wore "high costume," which included Victorian suits and dresses and military clothing worn with appropriate irony. The central goal was to use fashion to express the ideal of individuality.

the American debate over the nature of the nude body was in asking the question "Why is nudity considered obscene?"

Feminism and Sexual Liberation

The sexual revolution of the 1960s was very different for men and women. While men experienced relaxed social restrictions and were, in many cases, freed from concerns about marriage and family responsibilities, women often found that their hippie mates still expected them to fill traditional spousal and maternal roles.

In theory, the hippie ethos was supposed to foster a more egalitarian view of sex roles. While hippie men wanted their women to be sexually open, spiritual, and adventurous, they also, in many cases, wanted their women to behave in traditional ways. "Although many hippie guys managed to avoid nine-to-five jobs," writes Alice Echols in *Shaky Ground*, "few hippie girls avoided housework. Baking, cooking, sewing, tending the children were a 'women's thing.'"[8] This was especially true in the case of hippie communes, where women were often expected to cook and clean for members of the commune. This was troubling for many women, who sought freedom from the constraints of society only to find that hippie men made the same demands. "Instead of undoing the deeply rooted sexual double standard," wrote Echols, "free love only masked it in counterculture pieties."[9]

For their part, the young women who left home to join the ranks of the hippies were taking an enormous risk, especially given a society that did not readily accept the equality or independence of women. Many young women suffered for their courageous experiments, ending up homeless, penniless, and sometimes victims of rape and/ or abuse.[10] However, the bravery of the women who traveled on their own despite the risk, and who shed their traditional roles to explore society on their own terms, cannot be understated. It was among these women that the roots of "second wave" feminism took hold.

In addition, while hippie men did little to empower feminism, the hippie desire to detach sexuality from reproduction was a necessary step in the development of the feminist movement. This was helped, in no small way, by the research conducted at clinics established by American feminist activist Margaret Sanger. It was in 1948, at a clinic established by Sanger, that the first birth-control pill was invented. By 1963 more than 2.5 million American women were taking "the Pill."[11] The birth-control pill allowed women to enjoy sex without the fear of motherhood and, though some feminists would later claim that the Pill reinforced patriarchal social relationships, it was one of the most important technological inventions in the history of feminism. The birth-control pill empowered women by giving them more control over their bodies and allowing them the freedom to separate sexuality and reproduction on their own terms.

Taken as a whole, the central message of hippie sexuality was choice. Having emerged from the consensus culture of the 1950s, hippies wanted to abandon the stigmatized ideas about sex they inherited from their parents. While humans had long engaged in sex for fun and pleasure, the hippies sought to make this attitude mainstream. The hippie vision of sexuality was never fully realized, but popular attitudes about sexuality changed significantly in the wake of the 1960s.

While other movements in support of open sexual expression preceded the hippies, the hippie movement was the first to gain international media attention. Some criticized or lampooned hippie sexual behavior as indiscriminate, unhygienic, and irresponsible, while others celebrated it as revolutionary and profound. The attention given to the counterculture allowed hippies to reach across cultural lines and convinced many Americans to reexamine their views on sex.

Masturbation

At a time when doctors had difficulty broaching the subject, hippies and feminist theorists were encouraging Americans to explore their potential for orgasmic experience through masturbation. Hip language flourished on the subject, as they attempted to spread the idea that masturbation should be an expression of "self love" and not a shameful secret.

Notes

1. David Smith Allyn, *Make Love, Not War: The Sexual Revolution, an Unfettered History* (New York: Little, Brown, 2000), 5.
2. David Robins Pountain, *Cool Rules: Anatomy of an Attitude* (London: Reaktion Books, 2000), 79.
3. Timothy Miller, *The '60s Communes: Hippies and Beyond* (Syracuse, NY: Syracuse University Press, 1999), 202.
4. Allyn, *Make Love, Not War*, 116.
5. Ibid., 101.
6. Timothy Miller, *The Hippies and American Values* (Knoxville: University of Tennessee Press, 1991), 60.
7. Ruth Barcan, *Nudity: A Cultural Anatomy* (Gordonsville, VA: Berg Publishing, 2004), 776.
8. Alice Echols, *Shaky Ground: The '60s and Its Aftershocks* (New York: Columbia University Press, 2002), 34.
9. Ibid.
10. Dominick Cavallo, *A Fiction of the Past: The Sixties in American History* (New York: Macmillan, 2001), 140.
11. Gerard J. DeGroot, *The Sixties Unplugged: A Kaleidoscopic History of a Disorderly Decade* (Cambridge, MA: Harvard University Press, 2008), 40.

CHAPTER THREE

Drugs and the Search for Enlightenment

The Good Dope

As Timothy Miller pointed out in *The Hippies and American Values*, hippies made a distinction between "dope" and "drugs." While using dope—including those substances considered "natural" like marijuana, LSD, psilocybin, peyote, and mescaline—was considered a positive, natural form of recreation and even personal/spiritual exploration, hippies felt that drugs—including "synthetic" substances like heroin, cocaine, barbiturates, and methamphetamines—had a negative influence on the mind and body. "Substances that were perceived as expanding consciousness were good." wrote Miller. "Things that made the user dumb were bad."[1]

Despite the distinction between *good* dope and *bad* drugs, many used both in the pursuit of the hip lifestyle. Drugs, specifically amphetamines, heroin, and cocaine, claimed the lives of some of the era's biggest stars, including Jim Morrison, Janis Joplin, and Jimi Hendrix. Emerging from the sixties, the idea that drugs are "bad" is still shared by a vast majority of Americans, while the moral and ethical status of dope is still very much an issue of debate.

The Gallup Organization, for instance, has been measuring American attitudes on the legalization of marijuana since 1969 and has found that support for legalization increased from 12 percent in 1969 to 36 percent in 2005.[2] The Rasmussen Organization released

A hippie expresses her belief that drugs are not as harmful as war. (© 2009 Robert Altman. Used by permission. Appears in Robert Altman, The Sixties *[Santa Monica Press, 2007].)*

the results of a survey conducted in 2009, indicating that approximately 40 percent of U.S. citizens supported legalization.[3] Changing attitudes about marijuana led to the development of a "medical marijuana" industry and, as of 2008, 10 states allowed limited marijuana use for persons suffering from legitimate medical issues. While there is no similar movement to legalize LSD and other psychogenic compounds, numerous studies have found that Americans consider hallucinogens less dangerous and less of a "problem" than "hard drugs" like cocaine, heroin, and methamphetamines.

In the hippie communities of Haight-Ashbury and Greenwich Village, the use of dope was widespread. Marijuana, LSD, and other psychedelics were widely available on the street and were held in high esteem by a population in which the use of dope was an acceptable form of recreation, a form of resistance against the laws of the establishment, and a symbol of the hippies' association with an evolving worldview.

Dope culture expanded rapidly in the mid-1960s, fueled by the perception that many hippie icons, musicians, and other social figures used dope to enhance their creativity. To give one of many examples, the story of how singer Bob Dylan introduced the members of the British rock band the Beatles to marijuana in 1964, and the resulting effect on the Beatles' music, was evidence to many followers that marijuana was fuel for the imagination.[4]

According to Gallup polls, the number of Americans who reported having "tried" marijuana increased from 4 to 24 percent between 1969 and 1977. The trend decelerated in the 1970s, but the drug's popularity continued to rise as Gallup reported in 1999 that the percentage of the population admitting to experimentation with marijuana had increased to 34 percent.[5]

Spiritual Dope

While celebrity advocacy convinced many hippies to give dope a chance, there was another side to dope culture: spiritual and cultural leaders who advocated drug use as a tool for enlightenment. The most famous was former Harvard professor Timothy Leary, who was often derogatively called an "acid guru" for his widely publicized promotion of LSD as a spiritual aid.

The history of LSD also fueled the drug's popularity. Invented in 1938 by chemical researcher Albert Hofmann, who accidentally discovered that the substance had psychoactive properties after he spilled a small amount on his hand, LSD was initially hailed as a type of psychological cure-all with the potential to treat ailments like alcoholism, schizophrenia, and manic-depressive (bipolar) disorders. Before national prohibition, a host of celebrities and prominent artists were "treated" with medical LSD, including actors Cary Grant and Jack Nicholson and writer Aldous Huxley.

LSD remained legal until the mid-1960s, when growing use among the counterculture gave legislators the leverage they needed to demand prohibition, on a state-by-state basis. After several states passed prohibition laws, the federal government followed suit with the Drug Abuse Control Amendment of 1965, which prohibited all substances with hallucinogenic properties.[6]

Leary knew the history of LSD and firmly believed, as many psychologists once had, that LSD was a powerful psychological tool. To Leary, however, the substance's psychedelic effects were the key to the drug's benefit, rather than a side effect of the compound's chemical structure.

Acid, Leary believed, could destroy the culturally created façade that dominated the mind, allowing the user to see the world from a new perspective, one similar to the pure state of sense and experience that exists before social indoctrination, the state from which a newborn child presumptively views its environment. As described by Gerard DeGroot in *The Sixties Unplugged*, "LSD acts by temporarily dismissing the sentries guarding the gates of consciousness. The

---

Bad Trips

A "bad trip," or unpleasant psychedelic experience, occurred when users were unable to cope psychologically with the intensity of the experience. LSD inventor Albert Hofmann had the first recorded bad trip when he experimented on himself and experienced a sensation that he was surrounded by "demons" who intended to do him harm.

unprotected brain is invaded by a mode of unprocessed stimuli on which it is unable to impose logic."[7]

Leary claimed that LSD was inherently spiritual, intensely sensual, and even revolutionary. The power of LSD was that it allowed the individual to examine his or her life from a new perspective and, often, to come away feeling positively changed by the experience. Leary also believed that LSD was a powerful tool for expanding the potential for love and physical pleasure. As he said in an interview with *Playboy*, reprinted in his book *The Politics of Ecstasy*, "The three inevitable goals of an LSD session are to discover and make love with God, to discover and make love with yourself, and to discover and make love with a woman."[8]

Leary and others, who believed that dope was spiritual, organized churches and cults that used dope as part of their spiritual process. "Some evoked deep mystical religious experience;" wrote Miller, "others simply amounted to attempts to get around the drug laws. Some were deadly serious; some were whimsically lighthearted. Collectively they were one of the quainter byways of hip."[9]

Some churches attempted to emulate the ritual use of dope, as practiced by some North and South American indigenous tribes who use mescaline, peyote, and other substances in sacred rituals, while others preferred a more ambiguous form of spiritual association, borrowing from Eastern and Western spiritual traditions. The connection between dope and Eastern spirituality was in many ways fueled by the testimony of leaders like Allen Ginsberg and Richard "Ram Dass" Alpert, who were themselves proponents of Eastern spirituality and avid dope users.[10]

Fighting the Law

The use of dope was sanctioned by the "if it feels good . . ." principle, but prohibited by mainstream ethics and sometimes legal sanctions. Some hippies reveled in dope culture precisely because it was a form of rebellion but, in the end, many paid a hefty price for disregarding the law. Timothy Leary and Ken Kesey, who publicly flouted the drug laws, spent years running from warrants for drug possession, and both men spent short stints in prison. Many hippies, like Kesey and Leary, also paid a price for rebellion, with hundreds spending periods from days to years imprisoned on drug charges.

As a whole, the hippies believed that the government should not have the right to impose laws on consensual activities. The standard argument was that the government had no right to tell people what to do with their bodies, whether it was taking drugs or having sex. Dope fans argued that dope use only harmed the user and was, therefore, not an issue for governmental concern. While the hippies were not the first subculture to resist the curtailment of consensual crime, they brought the issue to the forefront of society.

One natural outgrowth of this "revolutionary" opposition was the movement to legalize marijuana. Modern organizations, like the National Organization for the Reform of Marijuana Laws (NORML) have their roots in early organizations like LeMar (Legalize Marijuana) International, which was started in 1964 and headed by hippie-era icons Allen Ginsberg and Ed Sanders.[11]

The popularity of dope among the hippies had the opposite effect in mainstream society. Fears that the morals of "decent" society were eroding in a puff of pot smoke gave fuel to the campaign to prohibit intoxicating substances. The government used the fear of the populace to push its own agenda and created propaganda to spread anti-drug messages.

The Federal Bureau of Narcotics (FBN), which had been lobbying for increased prohibitions against marijuana since the 1930s, promoted the idea that marijuana could lead to indiscriminant violence and to the use of other drugs. Despite having no reliable evidence to support its claims, the FBN spread fabricated reports of marijuana users committing murder and turning, helplessly, into heroin addicts. Incited to panic, the public urged lawmakers to take action and the penalties for marijuana sale and possession became increasingly punitive.[12]

As dope paranoia spread, the public became involved, helping to disseminate and in some cases create antidrug propaganda. Gerard DeGroot cites one example from 1968, wherein several newspapers reported a spurious story relayed by an employee of the Pennsylvania Institute for the Blind, who said the institute was caring for six young patients who were struck blind after staring at the sun under the influence of LSD. When the truth was revealed, the employee admitted to having conjured the story because he was concerned about the effects of drugs on society.[13]

Dope Culture

The vast majority of hippies were merely recreational users, but the demand for drugs created an economic niche for a hippie drug-dealing industry. While hippies sometimes purchased their dope from outside the community, they were more comfortable purchasing from dealers who were themselves hippies. In addition, the hippies created their own conventions, language, and traditions regarding the use of their favorite drugs. From "bad trips" to "bogarting" a joint, hippie jargon flourished on the subject of recreational drugs.

In sociologist Sherri Cavan's groundbreaking 1972 book *Hippies of the Haight*, she described the marijuana industry in San Francisco, including the process of selling marijuana as an occupation. According to Cavan, hippies accepted that they needed to purchase their drugs, but felt that the act of purchasing the drugs was itself contrary to hippie values, which opposed "buying into" the capitalist system. Hippies in the Haight would therefore have preferred to trade marijuana or have it given to them as an act of kindness by a fellow who shared their view of the world.

There was also a distinctly dark side to dope culture. Many hippies became dependent on drugs, especially alcohol and heroin, and fatal overdoses became increasingly common in the late 1960s. Some also used drugs as a form of escapism, avoiding their problems until they grew into serious issues. The potential for drug use to become a

---

Monday Night Class

In the mid-1960s, San Francisco State Professor Steve Gaskin began holding Monday night lectures at the Family Dog auditorium, on subjects ranging from LSD therapy to community involvement. Gaskin's lectures were attended by more than 1,500 students and became a primary gathering place for hippies. Gaskin later formed "The Farm," one of the longest-lasting communes in America.

social and psychological handicap doubtlessly hindered many young hippies from achieving their goals.

With the belief that dope was an avenue to enlightenment came the potential for abuse. During the "acid tests," for instance, hundreds of partygoers were given LSD with no warning and no consent. Unexpectedly exposed to the powerful psychoactive properties of the drug, many individuals were consumed by an experience they were not prepared to endure. Those who chose not to use drugs were sometimes ostracized from the community. "Like heathens judged by a peculiarly bigoted religion," wrote DeGroot, "those who did not indulge were cast from the kingdom."[14]

Drugs and hippie culture were inextricably linked, both in the realities of daily life and in the public imagination, which would continue to conflate the two long after the era ended. Whether taken for fun, political rebellion, or spiritual discovery, dope was both fuel and folly in hippie culture. As the former hippies grew into adults and had children of their own, American attitudes toward drug use began to change. The legacy of the hippie obsession with dope is most potently visible in the modern acceptance of some recreational drugs. While marijuana was once considered as dangerous as heroin, American pop culture has now learned to make light of the subject.

Notes

1. Timothy Miller, *The Hippies and American Values* (Knoxville: University of Tennessee Press, 1991), 25.
2. Joseph Carol, "Who Supports Marijuana Legalization," Gallup Organization, http://www.gallup.com/poll/19561/Who-Supports-Marijuana-Legalization.aspx (accessed November 1, 2008).
3. Rasmussen Reports. "40% Say Marijuana Should Be Legalized, http://www.rasmussenreports.com/public_content/lifestyle/general_lifestyle/february_2009/40_say_marijuana_should_be_legalized.
4. Sheila Weller, *Girls Like Us: Carole King, Joni Mitchell, and Carly Simon—and the Journey of a Generation* (New York: Simon and Schuster, 2008), 176.
5. Jennifer Robinson, "Who Smokes Pot? You May Be Surprised," Gallup Organization, July 16, 2002, http://www.gallup.com/poll/6394/Who-Smoked-Pot-May-Surprised.aspx (accessed November 1, 2008).
6. Albert Hofmann, *LSD My Problem Child: Reflections on Sacred Drugs, Mysticism, and Science* (Ben Lomond, CA: Multidisciplinary Association for Psychedelic Studies, 2005).

7. Gerard J. DeGroot, *The Sixties Unplugged: A Kaleidoscopic History of a Disorderly Decade* (Cambridge, MA: Harvard University Press, 2008), 208.

8. Timothy Leary, *The Politics of Ecstasy* (Berkeley, CA: Ronin Publishing, 1998), 128.

9. Timothy Miller, *The Hippies and American Values* (Knoxville: University of Tennessee Press, 1991), 31.

10. DeGroot, *The Sixties Unplugged*, 214.

11. Martin Booth, *Cannabis: A History* (New York: Macmillan, 2005), 254.

12. Richard J. Bonnie and Charles H. Whitebread, *The Marijuana Conviction: A History of Marijuana Prohibition in the United States* (New York: Lindesmith Center, 1999), 230–50.

13. DeGroot, *The Sixties Unplugged*, 213.

14. Ibid.

CHAPTER FOUR

Rock & Roll

In the book *Debating the 1960s*, the authors assert, "Even more than sex and psychedelic drugs, rock and roll distinguished the New Culture as a rebellion of the young."[1] While sex and drugs were tools of rebellion and an avenue through which the hippies challenged authority, the rock music of the sixties was a phenomenon unique to the time; it was emerging from and fueling the youth revolution. "Dope usually involved inward experiences," wrote Miller. "Liberated sex in most cases involved interpersonal relationships on a one-to-one basis. Rock, however, was communal, and thus it provided a medium for cultural communication."[2]

The Roots of Rock

One of the defining factors in the evolution of 1960s rock was the racial integration of American music, largely at the hands of radio disc jockeys like Cleveland's Alan Freed and Memphis's "Daddy-O" Dewey Phillips, who ran the *Red, Hot, and Blue* radio program. Phillips, whom DeGroot called "an irrepressible force in the racial integration of popular music," played white music and "race music" on his

---

Electric Guitar

While hippie rockers like Jimi Hendrix became famous for their guitar artistry, most of the techniques they used, even their methods of combining dance with guitar playing, were developed by blues musicians of the previous generation. The Who guitarist Pete Townsend's famous windmill strum, for instance, was first performed by gospel singer Rosetta Tharpe.

---

program, introducing white audiences to landmark African American artists like T-Bone Walker and Rosetta Tharpe.[3]

In its infancy, American rock was largely an attempt to imitate the energetic sounds of African American artists, as singers like Elvis Presley and Jerry Lee Lewis integrated blues and gospel into pop compositions. Presley and others like him found a way to make the blues sound palatable to white audiences and, as a result, rhythm and blues (R&B) found a new, young, white, affluent audience. Further fueled by the simultaneous emergence and popularization of the transistor radio, sales of blues records skyrocketed.[4]

By the early sixties, "doo-wop" rock was the popular sound in cities like Chicago, Philadelphia, New York, and Los Angeles. The youth of the late 1950s and early 1960s transformed this pre-rock music into a national phenomenon, and the recording industry, as well, attained previously unimagined levels of prosperity. As the popularity of the new rock sound grew in America, it was also exported to Europe and Latin America. In the urban areas of Britain, a flowering of young, rock-pop bands began to emerge.

The British Invasion

Across the Atlantic, George Harrison, John Lennon, Paul McCartney, and Ringo Starr, four young men from Liverpool, England, who would form one of the most influential rock bands in music history, were listening to the sounds emerging from the United States. Before they were the "Beatles," the four called themselves the "Moondogs," a name they pulled from DJ Alan Freed's *Moondog Rock and Roll House Party Show*, on WINS Radio in New York, one of the first all-rock, live radio shows in the nation.[5]

While not an American phenomenon, the evolution of the Beatles provides an interesting timeline to the sixties as a whole. When they came to America, the Beatles were the forerunners and chief architects of a musical movement that would later be called the "British Invasion." As the era changed, the Beatles consistently ranked as musical and cultural innovators, evolving from pop to psychedelic rock to singer/songwriters, as those same trends were rippling through the U.S. music scene.

The Beatles entered the British pop scene in 1960, and by 1963 had gained such enormous popularity that the media had given the phenomenon a name: "Beatlemania." By the time the Beatles reached the United States in February of 1964, they had already gained scores of fans. In addition, there were already dozens of Beatles imitators in the United States, many of which were created by studio executives to capitalize on the emerging trend. More than 73 million fans, a record audience, watched the Beatles perform on the *Ed Sullivan Show* in a now-famous February 9, 1964, concert.[6]

The Beatles arrived in America at a confluence, when dozens of distinct musical trends were merging at the intersection of art and culture. Fueled by the Beatles' popularity, record companies brought a slew of British bands to the United States. While some made only a minor impact, others, like the Rolling Stones and the Jimi Hendrix Experience, became major players in the developing musical movement.[7]

Psychedelic Rock Hits the Scene

The sounds that were exported to Britain through American radio came back across the Atlantic in a different form, which resonated with American youth. There were other influences at play as well. The folk revival of the 1950s, popularized in New York's Greenwich Village, had largely given way to rock music, but was also a predecessor and influence for rock bands who blended folk sentiments with their new sound. The student activist movement also played a role, as more and more American rock groups integrated political messages into their music.

By the mid-1960s, the new rock sound met the psychedelic revolution. The Beatles again served as a microcosm of the evolving music scene. By the release of their 1966 album *Revolver*, it was clear that the Beatles' sound and image were changing. It was widely known that the Beatles began experimenting with LSD and marijuana in 1965 and, though they denied that drugs influenced their music, their new sound was clearly more in keeping with the emerging psychedelic aesthetic.

The following year, the Beatles released *Sergeant Pepper's Lonely Hearts Club Band*, which contained a number of songs that seemed, to fans at least, to have veiled references to drug use. The most explicit was the song "Lucy in the Sky with Diamonds," a song rife with flowing lyrics, strange sound effects, and bizarre, dreamlike imagery. Some contested that the title of the song was an acronym for LSD.

While the Beatles denied these rumors, few were convinced. It was clear from their public appearances that the "Fab Four," as they were sometimes called, were now wearing their hair even longer and adorning themselves in psychedelic clothing. The popular perception that their songs promoted drug use was so strong that some states banned the Beatles from radio stations.[8]

While some rock bands used implied references to drug use and sexuality, a host of underground bands in the Haight-Ashbury were creating a new breed of rock that would leave little doubt that drugs and sex were integral parts of the American music scene. Most of the Haight-Ashbury bands got their start at small venues around San Francisco or in other West Coast hippie enclaves. By 1967 some of the Haight bands were beginning to attract nationwide attention.

Psychedelic Lighting

Psychedelic lighting was developed to accompany Beatnik poetry recitals but reached its peak in the mid-sixties as an accompaniment for psychedelic rock concerts. A typical technique was to shine lights through plates filled with dyed oils and water, thereby creating an undulating blob of color that seemed to move with the music.

Bands like Big Brother and the Holding Company, Jefferson Airplane, and the Grateful Dead emerged from the Haight-Ashbury scene with a genuinely new sound, blending country, protest rock, British pop, and R&B. The sound was loud and disorganized, and in many ways reflected the myriad influences and desires of the hippies who migrated from around the country to take part in the youth movement. Some of the new bands wrote lyrics with explicit or graphic references to drugs and sexuality, clearly establishing the new sound as rebellious. The rock bands often utilized feedback, spatial distortion through stereo recording, and a number of cutting-edge studio effects to create a "hallucinatory" vibe that gave the music its name, "psychedelic rock."[9]

This type of music was made for and enhanced by drugs, and many of the musicians who pioneered the sound regularly performed under the influence. The concerts and gatherings became the primary place for hippies to get together and mingle, away from the judgment of the mainstream. Soon, inclusion in hippie culture was tied to the music, as those who were considered "real hippies" were expected to "know" rock music.

The rock sound of the Haight spread around the world and became a clear expression of the youth movement. While hippies rebelled against many things, their music was something they created. It was a symbol that hippie culture was not simply opposition, but also profoundly creative, innovative, and unique.

The Festivals

The music festivals of the sixties, including the infamous Woodstock Festival, were some of the more unique and lasting developments of hippie culture. The festival scene flowered in San Francisco, where the large hippie population and favorable climate created the perfect setting for staging outdoor concerts. From small gatherings to massive carnivals that filled Golden Gate Park, hippies flocked to the festivals to enjoy music, to dance, and to socialize in an environment where nearly everyone shared the same values and, often, the same substances.

In *The Hippies and American Values*, Miller said of the festivals, "They helped shape rock and provided the best opportunities for massive indulgence in the sacraments: dope, nudity, sex, rock, community."[10] In addition to popularizing the new rock music, festivals like the 1967 Human Be-In in Golden Gate Park were also gathering places for hippie intellectuals. Between musical performances, hippies would listen to speeches from political and spiritual leaders, poets, and activists. Activist-poet Allen Ginsberg and LSD guru Timothy Leary were two of many prominent speakers who attended the 1967 Be-In.[11]

Psychedelic rock bands like Big Brother and the Holding Company and the Jimi Hendrix Experience were perfect for the festival venues, where loose schedules allowed artists to improvise more freely, and even a "sloppy" performance would be appreciated by fans who were excited simply to take part in the celebration. For the bands that played at the festivals, it was a chance to share the stage with other musicians in the same movement, and many chose to collaborate, turning the stage into a "jam" with musicians from multiple bands feeding off one another.

In many ways, the music festivals were the culmination of hippie culture and hippie rock, but they also signaled the end of the golden age of hippies. Because of the huge turnouts, the festivals were afforded significant attention in the mainstream media, which both recruited new followers to the hippie scene and attracted intense scrutiny from authorities.

The Monterey International Pop Festival of 1967, for instance, introduced national audiences to Haight-Ashbury rock bands like Janis Joplin and the Grateful Dead and led, more than any other event, to the Summer of Love, in which nearly 100,000 migrants flocked to San Francisco to join the hippie scene. For many of the "old hippies" living in Haight-Ashbury, this was the end of true hippie-ism. For those newly arriving in the Haight, however, it was the peak of the experience—thousands of hippies living together in an environment where hippie ideals could be freely practiced.[12]

By 1969, the immense popularity of the hippie scene made staging festivals a logistical nightmare. Media and critics blasted the Woodstock Music and Art Fair, which occurred on a farm in Bethel, New York, from August 15 to 18, 1969, for the myriad problems that plagued the event, including insufficient sanitation, food, and medical services. At the Altamont, California, concert a few weeks later, a fan was knifed to death by Hells Angels security guards during the

Hippies dance in ecstasy at one of the popular outdoor venues. (© 2009 Robert Altman. Used by permission. Appears in Robert Altman, The Sixties *[Santa Monica Press, 2007].)*

Rolling Stones set. An article in the *Berkeley Barb* described the concert simply: "Someone was knifed to death. Lots of people were beaten. Love and peace were f***ed by the Hells Angels in front of hundreds of thousands of people who did nothing."[13]

In the early 1970s, music fans around the world were shocked and saddened by the deaths of some of the era's most famous musicians, including Janis Joplin and Jimi Hendrix, both from drug overdoses. Joplin and Hendrix were symbols of the spirit that created the festival scene and their deaths were symbolic, for many, of the dangerous excesses of hippie culture. Though the festivals would continue in subsequent decades, they would never regain the same flavor achieved in the heyday of the hippie era.

The Singer/Songwriters

Mainstream popularity of psychedelic rock lasted for only a couple of years. By the end of 1969, a new breed of artists was coming to light, led by forerunners like James Taylor, Carly Simon, Cat Stevens, and Joni Mitchell. This was the beginning of the singer/songwriter era, which saw a decline in the popularity of noisy, energetic rock and an increasing focus on soft, introspective, acoustic music.[14] Some artists who took part in the psychedelic rock scene evolved into singer/songwriters, including John Lennon after the breakup of the Beatles in 1969.

While the crest of hippie rock had fallen, many of the artists who had helped to create the rock scene remained influential for decades. The Rolling Stones, who were British Invasion pioneers, and the Grateful Dead, who were leaders in the bluegrass rock movement, both continued touring and recording into the 21st century.

The singer/songwriters of the 1970s were a product of the sixties' music scene. Though they ultimately initiated a new era, some singer/songwriters, like Joni Mitchell and Joan Baez, were also prominent during the height of the hippie era, representing the softer, more emotional side of hippie culture. The singer-songwriters represented some of the most lasting effects of the hippies on pop culture. Where psychedelic rock was the musical expression of counterculture angst and rebellion, singer/songwriters were a musical reflection of the hippie focus on love, self expression, and artistic realization.

Notes

1. Michael W. Flamm and David Steigerwald, *Debating the 1960s: Liberal, Conservative, and Radical Perspectives* (Lanham, MD: Rowman and Littlefield, 2008), 65.
2. Timothy Miller, *The Hippies and American Values* (Knoxville: University of Tennessee Press, 1991), 74.
3. Gerard J. DeGroot, *The Sixties Unplugged: A Kaleidoscopic History of a Disorderly Decade* (Cambridge, MA: Harvard University Press, 2008), 23.
4. Ibid., 22.
5. Paul Friedlander, *Rock and Roll: A Social History* (New York: Westview Press, 1996), 80.
6. Ibid., 85.
7. Timothy E. Scheurer, *American Popular Music: Readings from the Popular Press* (Madison, WI: Popular Press, 1989), 132.
8. Friedlander, *Rock and Roll*, 90–93.

9. Michael Hicks, *Sixties Rock: Garage, Psychedelic, and Other Satisfactions* (Urbana: University of Illinois Press, 2000), 73–75.

10. Miller, *The Hippies*, 82.

11. Martin Torgoff, *Can't Find My Way Home: America in the Great Stoned Age, 1945–2000* (New York: Simon and Schuster, 2004), 206–30.

12. Friedlander, *Rock and Roll*, 196–97.

13. Miller, *The Hippies*, 83.

14. Friedlander, *Rock and Roll*, 101.

| # Politics and the Establishment

Hippie culture arose at a time of intense social conflict. A host of important issues were at the forefront of society, including the civil rights struggle, the Cold War and the war in Vietnam, and the nuclear disarmament movement. These and other national issues informed and inspired many hippies to take social action; however, political activism was not the central theme of hippie culture. Taken as a whole, hippies were sympathetic to the political causes of the era rather than intimately driven by them.[1]

Hippies arose in opposition to mainstream culture and, for this reason if no other, they opposed the establishment, from laws governing the use of recreational drugs to the conflict in Vietnam. The general philosophy of opposition meant that hippies were often willing to join protests, marches, and other political movements, but also that some hippies rejected the very idea that they *should* be politically active.

The New Left

The Vietnam conflict, which began in 1959 and was an offshoot of the ongoing Cold War, was one of the primary political issues of the

---

The Peace Symbol

The "peace symbol," as it is now known, was created to symbolize the British Campaign for Nuclear Disarmament (CDN), by combining the graphic representations of the semaphore (a type of long-range visual signaling performed with flags) signals for the letters N and D. The American civil rights movement later adopted the symbol and it took on a more generalized meaning of nonviolence.

1960s. Opposition to the Vietnam conflict, and U.S. military policy in general, was a major factor in the origin of a family of social movements that were grouped under the catchall term "New Left," a moniker borrowed from a letter written by sociologist C. Wright Mills entitled "Open Letter to the New Left."[2] Taking inspiration from Mills and other political theorists, the various political movements that made up the New Left shared central goals: to ignite a New Leftist movement in America, and to oppose right-wing dominance in American social and political policy.

Among the more prominent New Left organizations were the Students for a Democratic Society (SDS) and the Student Nonviolent Coordinating Committee (SNCC). These organizations opposed not only U.S. military policy but also U.S. civil rights policy and other prevalent political issues. Members primarily came from universities and colleges and they gathered in huge numbers at antiwar protests, civil rights marches, and anti–nuclear weapons demonstrations.[3]

When the SDS began falling apart in the late 1960s, some of the organization's former leaders banded together to form a far more radical organization they called the Weathermen, later called the Weather Underground. The Underground was determined to undermine what they saw as an unjust governmental system by any means, and, toward this end, they organized bombings and kidnappings and were implicated in several instances of murder.

Though the Weather Underground and the hippies occasionally crossed paths, as when members of the Underground participated in breaking hippie guru Timothy Leary out of prison in 1970, most hippies had little in common with the underground radicals. As with any counterculture movement, the Weather Underground represented an

Hundreds of hippies gather in the San Francisco Presidio for an antiwar demonstration. (© 2009 Robert Altman. Used by permission. Appears in Robert Altman, The Sixties *[Santa Monica Press, 2007].)*

extreme offshoot of the same political and social unrest that fueled the other, more moderate protest movements and, to a lesser extent, the counterculture as a whole.[4]

The hippies, and 1960s counterculture in general, encompassed a wide range of political types. While many hippies were sympathetic to the New Left, they did not necessarily consider themselves activists, and most members of the New Left did not consider themselves hippies. Some in the activist movement held the hippies in disdain for being self-absorbed and hedonistic, and criticized them for their luxuriant recreation in the face of widespread global suffering.[5] In some ways, however, the goals of the hippies and the New Left converged.

The Politics of Hippie-ism

One of the primary facets of hippie culture was a focus on "love." The hippies deified the very idea of "love," whether expressed in the emotional and/or sexual union between individuals or in the principle of universal love for humankind. At every hippie gathering, from the communes of the early 1960s to the Woodstock concert of 1969, one could find a spiritual/social leader expounding on the idea of love and its importance as a central tenet of life. The focus on love led to widespread hippie belief in nonviolence, and this convinced many hippies to support the antiwar movement and the civil rights struggle, creating a bridge between the hippies and the leftists.[6]

Another bridge between the New Left and the hippies was constructed over the issue of materialism. To the hippies, materialism and the pursuit of financial prosperity distracted from the higher goals of building communities and seeking personal fulfillment. To the New Left, the capitalist system in America was the motivation behind military aggression and the oppression of minorities.[7]

While the New Left opposed the way the U.S. government obtained and used its wealth, the hippie objection to materialism was far more idealistic, based on the idea that money is a meaningless commodity that is merely symbolic of a host of intangible assets.[8]

Hippies envisioned a world freed from the pursuit of wealth, where communities would provide for one another in the spirit of love and harmonious coexistence. However, analysts have often pointed out that most hippies came from privileged backgrounds and were therefore free to criticize the system from a risk-free vantage point. Free to dream about an idealistic world, hippies formed their political philosophy on the basis of antimaterialist sentiments, which brought them closer to the leftist radicals.

In contrast to the leftists, however, some hippies believed that participation in political action was tantamount to "buying in" to the

---

Lay It on Me

Hippies felt that sharing and trading were superior to using money, an evil remnant of the corrupt system. The ideal was to have someone "lay it on you," meaning to give you the thing you wanted without expectation of payment. Hippies sometimes criticized persons who seemed to have excess goods, marijuana, or other things, and refused to share.

establishment. A prevalent argument was that American culture had become corrupt and dysfunctional and that those in good conscience should "drop out" of society, adopting a lifestyle of complete abstinence from the conventions of the mainstream, including politics. To the dropouts, the political institution was only to be challenged when it directly interfered with the desire to "do one's own thing." In the words of hippie guru Timothy Leary in *Turn On, Tune In, Drop Out,* "we are free and independent, and we are absolved from all Allegiance to the United States Government and all governments controlled by the menopausal."[9]

While many activists considered the dropout mentality childish, Leary and other hippies took it seriously. As Leary envisioned it, dropping out was nothing less than a refusal to "play the game" of mainstream society and, if the movement was supported by a large number of people, could lead to a new world order in which individuals would be encouraged to engage in individualized explorations for the purpose of finding pleasure and fulfillment.[10] While this view may seem simplistic by modern standards, it must be remembered that hippie culture was, by and large, a rejection of mainstream American society rather than a response to the realities of global politics.[11]

At the intersection of the hippies and the New Left were groups like Jerry Rubin's Yippies, dedicated to political action as a means of gaining attention for the larger youth movement. Rubin's Yippies protested the Vietnam War, American materialism, and a host of other issues, often in unusual, provocative ways, like their decision to promote a pig as their candidate for the 1968 Democratic presidential nomination.

Some leftists criticized the Yippies, saying that their protests were more publicity stunts than substantive resistance. The Yippies believed, however, that any stunt that succeeded in increasing attention on the problems of society was a move in the right direction.[12] In terms of national impact, the Yippies and their antics became the lasting symbols of the hip political stance.

The Communal Experiment

The Oneida Community was not only an experiment in alternative forms of sexual union, but was also an early example of an "intentional community," also called a "commune." In the mid-1960s, many hippies were attracted to the idea of communal living, creating places where they could live the ideal hippie life, free from the rules of "straight" society. Unlike Oneida, many hippie communes were secular, based on agreements of mutual interest rather than allegiance to a spiritual code.

Historians generally agree that the first rural hippie commune was the settlement known as Drop City, established on the outskirts of Trinidad, Colorado, in 1965. The idea behind Drop City, which took the form of a collection of geodesic domes in the middle of an expanse of grass, was to create a self-sustaining environment where artists could live and cooperate in the production of new art and performance projects. The Drop City artists envisioned themselves as a utopian community living *within* a work of art.

One of the innovations of the hippie commune was the idea that individuals who chose to live in the communes accepted equal responsibility for all the duties and daily activities necessary to keep the community functioning. At Drop City, for instance, the founding members imagined the community as a "tribe," formed in a cooperative spirit where each individual surrendered a portion of his or her daily freedom for the good of the group, but without having to be told to do so. "There is no political structure in Drop City," founder Peter Rabbit said of the community. "Things work out; the cosmic forces mesh with people in a strange complex intuitive interaction."[13]

There is no accurate figure of how many alternative communities were founded in the 1960s and 1970s. Some historians estimate that there were thousands of such groups, both urban and rural. Many, however, lasted only a short time (one or two years was the average) because of poor planning and execution.[14]

The "communards," as residents of communes are called, usually came from middle-class, white, suburban neighborhoods, and many had difficulty adjusting to the communal life. The vast majority of communes disintegrated because of human relations issues ranging from disagreements over the dispensation of labor to simple personality clashes exacerbated by close proximity. Female communards, as mentioned earlier, often found that males expected them to be responsible for the bulk of the domestic duties, like cooking and cleaning, and this imbalance in expectations convinced many women to abandon the communes.[15]

Some rural communes were based on an agrarian model, wherein participants cooperated to cultivate some or all of the food they needed. In the eyes of many rural communards, living "off the land" was a simpler and more harmonious existence. Farming communes were a precursor of the "Back to the Land" movement of the 1970s, in which hundreds left urban areas in an attempt to "return" to a pre-industrial way of life. The Back to the Land movement was itself part of an evolving eco-consciousness in Europe and America, which ultimately led to the Green Revolution of the 1990s.

Because most communards had no prior experience with farming or the hard work it entails, agricultural communes were short-lived. Some urban communards also attempted to reach some level of self-subsistence, either by growing food in urban gardens or creating systems of barter to obtain the colony's basic needs. It was more common for urban communards to work outside the commune, however, contributing a portion of their income to the communal pot.

One of the most successful agricultural communes was the Twin Oaks Community, which was founded in 1967 in Louisiana County, Virginia. The founding members had no experience with farming but managed to learn as the commune developed. Twin Oaks based its social structure on a model of egalitarian cooperation and, unlike many communes, women and men shared equally in all activities. In addition, anyone wishing to join the commune had to agree to share any income he or she personally earned with all other members of the commune. Twin Oaks was still active as of 2009, making it one of the most enduring communes in America.[16]

Hippie communes differed from other types of communes in a number of ways. While some hippie communes were religious, they were more often based on some form of "alternative" religion, rather than Christianity or Judaism. In addition, many hippies used a modified "tribal" structure for their communes, usually based loosely on the Native American example.

The hippies also imagined other, more unusual, types of communes, like the Hog Farm Collective, which is one of the oldest extant hippie communes. Before settling in rural California and assuming a standard agricultural communal model, the Hog Farm

> ## Modern Primitives
>
> The hippies often deified Native American tribal societies for their perceived harmony with the environment and simple lifestyles. While the fascination was largely a fad, the hippies did manage to reinvigorate the public debate over the treatment of Native Americans and many hippies joined political movements to free Native American political prisoners.

Collective, under the leadership of founding member Hugh Romney, was a "traveling commune." Romney, his family, and fellow communards traveled the country and abroad, visiting communities along the way where they helped to manage and prepare for outdoor music festivals.

As the urban hippie scene began to deteriorate, many of the more committed hippies decided that cities were incompatible with the ideal hippie life. Sociologist Sherri Cavan, who studied hippie culture in Haight-Ashbury and elsewhere, noted that many former urban hippies migrated to rural areas where they either became "villagers," meaning they moved as individuals or single families into small towns, or they joined some form of commune.

Though communards constituted only a small minority of the hippie population, the communal life proved one of the most lasting and effective methods of realizing the hippie lifestyle. The longevity of the few communes remaining into the 21st century demonstrates that the hippie ideal is tenable under certain circumstances, even if it was difficult to fully realize within the context of mainstream culture.

The Dawn of Environmentalism

Another important facet of hippie political culture was the hippies' acceptance and promotion of environmentalism. From the serial publication of Rachel Carson's landmark environmental book *Silent Spring* in the June 1962 issue of the *New Yorker*, a new environmental age was born and members of both the New Left and the hippies were the first to openly support the environmental movement.[17]

Many hippies felt strongly about the natural environment, drawing inspiration from Native American and other indigenous philosophies rooted in the idea that humans are inextricably tied to nature. Few hippies recognized the extent of environmental decay that would ultimately give way to 21st-century concerns like species extinction and global warming; rather, they saw proximate signs that humankind was exerting an "unnatural" dominion over nature and felt that this was a situation that needed to be remedied.[18]

While the hippies weren't responsible for building the environmental movement, their support, coupled with an increasing interest in environmental science within the academic community, brought about government action. Though President Kennedy considered environmental protection a minor concern, public support drove the government to create important environmental legislation that led to, among other innovations, the Clean Air Act of 1963 and the Endangered Species Act of 1966.[19]

For many hippies, the extent of their involvement in politics was resisting the attempts of the police or other authorities to interfere in their attempts to have a good time. For others, questioning the social order led to a desire to become active, to join a movement, and to force a change. In many ways, the primary political impact of the hippies was their willingness to question the social order and experiment with new ways of behaving. While the leftist radicals fought for political change, the hippies simply asked themselves and each other, "Why are things the way they are?" and decided to do things their own way.

Notes

1. Thomas G. Blomberg and Karol Lucken, *American Penology: A History of Control* (Piscataway, NJ: Aldine Transaction, 2000), 134–35.
2. Arnold J. Heidenheimer, *Political Corruption: Readings in Comparative Analysis* (Piscataway, NJ: Transaction Publishers, 1978).
3. Nigel Young, *An Infantile Disorder?: The Crisis and Decline of the New Left* (New York: Routledge, 1977), 24–30.
4. Jeremy Varon, *Bringing the War Home: The Weather Underground, the Red Army Faction, and Revolutionary Violence in the Sixties and Seventies* (Berkeley: University of California Press, 2004).

5. Rebecca E. Klatch, *A Generation Divided: The New Left, the New Right, and the 1960s* (Berkeley: University of California Press, 1999), 135–40.

6. Timothy Miller, *The Hippies and American Values* (Knoxville: University of Tennessee Press, 1991), 104–5.

7. Lewis Yablonsky, *The Hippie Trip* (El Segundo, CA: Pegasus, 1968).

8. Miller, *The Hippies*, 111.

9. Timothy Leary, *Turn On, Tune In, Drop Out* (San Francisco: Ronin Publishing, 1999), 145.

10. Ibid., 6.

11. Miller, *The Hippies*, 109–10.

12. David Farber, *Chicago '68* (Chicago: University of Chicago Press, 1994), 210–13.

13. Fred Turner, *From Counterculture to Cyberculture* (Chicago: University of Chicago Press, 2006), 15.

14. Timothy Miller, *America's Alternative Religions* (Albany, NY: SUNY Press, 1995), 371.

15. Eva Etzioni-Halevy. *Social Change: The Advent and Maturation of Modern Society* (New York: Taylor and Francis, 1981), 233.

16. Barbara Goodwin, *The Philosophy of Utopia* (New York: Taylor and Francis, 2001), 157.

17. Gerard J. DeGroot, *The Sixties Unplugged: A Kaleidoscopic History of a Disorderly Decade* (Cambridge, MA: Harvard University Press, 2008), 111–14.

18. Timothy Miller, *The '60s Communes: Hippies and Beyond* (Syracuse, NY: Syracuse University Press, 1999).

19. DeGroot, *The Sixties Unplugged*, 113–14.

Conclusion

Who Were the Hippies?

There is no such thing as a "hippie."

The first time the word was uttered might have been in the smoky parlors of New York's jazz houses in the 1940s or 1950s. The predominantly African American regulars created a plethora of unique words to describe their world, including the descriptor "hip," meaning "knowledgeable about the latest trends." Linguists are uncertain about the etymology, but some have suggested that "hip" was derived from a West African word, "hipi," meaning "to have one's eyes open."[1] Those who were hip were called "hipsters" a term that was adapted sometime in the 1950s to create the diminutive "hippies."

The term hit the mainstream in the 1960s, after a small number of journalists began using it to describe the counterculture in San Francisco. From there, it was adopted by the conventional media and spread across the country. By the late 1960s the word had been permanently linked to the counterculture. The hippies themselves never embraced the term "hippie," though they did agree that they were "hip."

The word "hip" was exceedingly common in the counterculture and many hippie writers and intellectuals even called their society the "hip world." The word became a code for anything that was acceptable within their culture, from music and art to attitudes about life and society. The phrase "I'm hip" was an all-purpose term signifying understanding and belonging within the subculture. It was the hippies' love for the word that most likely gave the media the idea to call them "hipsters" and "hippies."

Like the earlier usage, the media used "hippies" to describe kids who knew about, and were taking part in, the latest cultural and social trends. They identified hippies by their choices in fashion, recreation, politics, and music. This is the definition that is still most commonly used—a culture of recreational drug use, antiwar protests, psychedelic rock music, and characteristic fashion trends like paisley-patterned clothing and tie-dyeing. On a more general level, the hippies were identified as proponents of a liberal lifestyle that included, but was not limited to, the pursuit of personal freedom.

In the decades that followed, two views of hippies emerged. In the popular view, hippies were members of the liberal, bohemian counterculture, while historians and scholars have often treated hippies as members of a legitimate "social movement," arising as a backlash to mainstream culture of the 1950s and early 1960s. The latter definition stems largely from the hippies' participation in the broader youth rebellion of the 1960s, including the civil rights struggle, debates about freedom of assembly and expression, and the anti-Vietnam movement.

Both the scholarly and popular definitions are insufficient to capture the reality of the hippie phenomenon. Calling the hippies a "youth movement" is as flawed as describing hippies as people who wore headbands and circular sunglasses while smoking marijuana. Sixties counterculture was part profound social change and part pedestrian posturing and, while some believed passionately in changing the world order, others followed the trends simply because it was the "cool" thing to do.

The idea of the "hippie" was created from outside the culture itself and served primarily to pigeonhole a diverse group of young people who took part in the counterculture. In most cases, the terms used to describe the counterculture were levied from the other side of the cultural divide and intended to reduce, condemn, and criticize the youth of the era. Within the counterculture, the hippies created their own labels for those who were outside of their world, calling them "squares" or "straights," terms meant to convey the "rigidly conventional" attitudes of the mainstream set. The cultural landscape of the country was a battleground, with the hip kids on one side and the straight world on the other.[2]

Though they defied definition, the impact of the hippies, and 1960s counterculture in general, on American society is undeniable. The underground permeated and altered mainstream culture so quickly and to such an extent that there were few facets of society in the 1970s that did not bear the mark of 1960s' youth culture.

The Impact of the Hippies

Hippies and Globalization

According to one take on American history, the beginning of the Cold War (~1935–1940) was the end of political "isolationism" in the United States and the beginning of a period some historians describe as "internationalism."[3] According to this view, it was then that the U.S. government realized it was necessary, even essential, for the nation to become strongly engaged in international politics. The struggle to define a new role for the United States in the global sphere brought the U.S. government into a protracted struggle against the forces of communism, then viewed as the only political system with the might and influence to threaten the "American way of life."[4]

In the 1950s the Cold War manifested in the United States as an intense paranoia about the insidious influence of communism in the domestic environment, sometimes known as the "Red Scare." As the government began turning a suspicious eye toward its own constituents, hoping to ferret out communist sympathizers and potential agents of espionage, the populace fell under a veil of cultural repression, censorship, and uncertainty. Individual freedom, whether speech, association, education, or artistic expression, was curtailed by government policy and self-censorship on the part of institutions and individuals who feared being identified as communist sympathizers.[5] For fear of being seen as "un-American," Americans shunned anything and everything that was not home-grown, from foreign music and art to forming friendships and associations with immigrants.

The 1960s saw the breakdown of the cultural isolation imposed by Cold War social repression. Where the Beats led the way with their radical challenge to conformist society, the hippies took the rebellion further afield. For the hippies, exploring, celebrating, and emulating foreign behaviors, lifestyles, and philosophies was the *hip* thing to do.

In sharp contrast to the government's internationalist agenda, intended to establish the American dominance over its perceived enemies, hippie internationalism was grassroots. To the hippies, the American "system" was at the root of society's problems and, therefore, exploring other ways of living and thinking was an avenue to a different (and hopefully superior) way of life.

The hippie hunger for things "un-American" led to an increase in the import of international culture. Radio and television stations began producing international music and news programs, while American merchants hungrily imported goods, art, and literature from other countries. More than at any previous period, Americans were aware of what was going on in other parts of the world, from the struggles for independence in Africa to the student revolutions in Europe.

Throughout most of the sixties, television was still largely conservative, and the major networks primarily catered to mainstream tastes. However, televised news brought the Vietnam conflict and other international events into the American living room and marked a turning point in American consciousness regarding international affairs. Some social theorists imagined that television would lead to a new "global culture," in which all countries were linked by sound and video, thereby ushering in a new age of connectivity.[6] Television, for all its faults and failings, did help to create stronger connections across international lines, and this phenomenon deepened with the onset of the computer and Internet age.

While the hippies were avid consumers of international culture, the artistic output of the counterculture was also popular with foreign audiences. The psychedelic rock sound, for instance, found its way into Europe, South America, and elsewhere. One of the most prominent examples is the exchange between the United States and Brazil.

In the late sixties, Brazil, like the United States, was in the midst of a youth revolution. Hundreds of Brazilians participated in protesting oppressive state policies that limited speech and expression as the government passed through a number of short-lived military dictatorships. Young Brazilian musicians, hearing American and British music through imported records and radio broadcasts, found something they identified with in the rebellious sounds of the psychedelic rock. From this, pioneers like Jorge Ben and Caetano Veloso "cannibalized" the new sound and blended it with Brazilian bossa nova and samba, creating a new wave of Brazilian music called the "tropicalia movement."[7]

The export of hippie music to Brazil was only one example of how innovations created in the counterculture found their way to a global audience. Hippie fashion also spread; from the shapes of sunglass frames to hairstyles and fabric choices, the youth in America created a culture with global appeal.

The 1960s was also an era of "road tripping," and many hippies reveled in the joys of nomadic travel across the United States, stopping briefly to check out some intriguing scene before moving on. Some of the more adventurous hippies traveled and lived abroad, exploring, among other places, India, Asia, and Europe.

Hippie wanderers, drifters, and expatriates helped to foster what would become a national fascination with the pleasures and mind-expanding benefits of international exploration. This coincided with a global increase in the popularity of jet travel, a trend that has continued unabated from the 1960s to the 21st century. The particular mode of travel that most appealed to the hippies, focusing on experience rather than consumerism, was a precursor to the "backpacking" fad among American college students and, later, the ecotourism movement of the 1990s.[8]

The hippies rejected nationalism, largely because most believed that the American system was flawed. Many imagined themselves as cosmopolitan and promoted the idea of global citizenship. This basic philosophical shift, in addition to an increased propensity for international travel, is an important consideration when evaluating the hippies' effect on the evolving American worldview.

The hippies marked an important point in the history of globalization—the blending of international cultures that is now recognized as one of the driving forces in the evolution of global culture. While modern examinations of globalization often focus on economic indicators, trade agreements, and the influence of the Internet, the hippies must also be acknowledged as products *and* agents of globalization.

Hippie Cars

Automaker Volkswagen's 1960s ads for the "Beetle" carried the slogan "Think small," which reversed the industry standard of presenting cars as status symbols. The minimization strategy was perfect for the emerging hippie market, capitalizing on the idea of doing one's own thing and focusing on utility rather than status.

Perhaps the greatest hippie contribution to globalization was that they brought their hunger for international culture back to the mainstream as they returned, albeit reluctantly, to conventional society.[9]

Assimilating the Hippies

Most hippies were kids or teenagers in the sixties, with an average age of 19, and most came from middle and upper-middle-class families. A consequence of this demographic feature is that most hippies had homes to return to when they left their counterculture communities. As a group, the hippies were also educated, at least to the high-school level, enabling them to find jobs and other roles within conventional society. Some historians have argued that it is inaccurate to describe the hippies as "returning" to the mainstream because, in contrast to revolutionary groups like the Black Panther Party and the Weather Underground, the hippies never fully abandoned the straight world. While the hippies favored the philosophy of antiestablishment thinkers, they were always avid consumers and active participants in commercial culture.[10]

Whether or not they left the mainstream, former hippies had been permanently altered by their participation in the counterculture, and many refused to relinquish their newfound values and ethics for the norms and folkways of their parents. As they took jobs, returned to the educational system, and raised their own children, the former hippies helped to define a *new* mainstream. Some started businesses and organizations aimed at maintaining counterculture ideals within conventional society. One example can be found in the establishment of educational institutions with a greater focus on personal development rather than standardized goals and measures of progress. Another example is the environmentally friendly consumer market, which by the 1990s resulted in national chains providing environmentally conscious and ethically responsible goods. The entire eco-consumer market must be seen as a product of the era of the hippies, who were the first generation of Americans to adopt widespread awareness about environmental decline.

The capitalist system eventually adjusted to the new consumer base, many of who had been part of hippie culture. Even in the early 1960s, just as the hippie trend was beginning to coalesce, advertisers were geared toward the teen market. It wasn't long before advertisers started using hippie slang, calling a pair of jeans "hip" or a new car "cool." Even the concepts of "revolution" and "rebellion" were reduced to slogans and catch phrases for companies marketing to current and former hippies.[11]

The children of the hippies, who grew up in the 1970s and 1980s, were also products of 1960s counterculture, though a generation removed. Many were raised in unconventional environments as the former hippies struggled with the question of how to bequeath the best of the counterculture, such as the concept of universal love, the importance of the individual, and freedom of expression, to the next generation. Some sociologists have argued that "Generation X" is a generation of cynics who rejected their parents' lifestyle as impractical and self-absorbed. The impact of Generation X must also be considered a consequence of the 1960s, as the generation arose partially in reaction to the failings and excesses of the hippies.[12]

The Individual and the Group

In a 1976 article for *New York* magazine, novelist Tom Wolfe criticized the American people as a population obsessed with itself, whose quest for self-awareness and personal fulfillment had all but erased the concepts of reciprocity and community involvement. He derisively labeled the 1970s the "'Me' decade," citing the breakdown of marriage, the popularity of self-centered modes of spirituality, and the pursuit of ecstasy at the expense of society.[13]

While some might view Wolfe's exposition as cynical criticism, the focus on the "individual" was an inescapable theme in hip culture and one of the legacies the hippies left to the next generation. However, the hippies were divided on the issue. While many believed a greater focus on the individual was warranted, perhaps in reaction to the "put society first" mentality that had been standardized since before the First World War, the hippies also liked the idea of community. Hip leaders at times advocated self-enlightenment and individual experience, but also called for unity and the cooperative creation of a new, collective culture that would supplant the old.[14]

The hippies were, in many ways, a culture of contradictions. They were attracted to the idea of individualism, as embodied in folk archetypes like the lone revolutionary and the solitary spiritual seeker. They were also fascinated by what they perceived as naturally occurring and harmonious groups, embodied in archetypes like the Native American tribe and the Buddhist monastery. Many rejected the idea that these concepts were at odds. After all, the revolutionary frees the people to live among them, and the spiritual seeker finds solace with like-minded monks. More than individualized happiness, hippies dreamed of creating a society in which the group did not obscure the individual, and where individual personalities combined to give the group strength and harmony.

There is little doubt, however, that the hip focus on individualized happiness had unforeseen consequences. Divorce rates, for instance, climbed to unprecedented levels, rising from 9 to 21 percent in the years from 1960 to 1990. There were a number of contributing factors to this statistic, including the "no fault" divorce laws and the Vietnam conflict; however, hip culture certainly facilitated the trend.[15] The willingness to divorce was part of the hippie rejection of the conventional social model, in which committing to country, family, and community was seen as the only morally permissible mode of existence. The hippies' individualism was an experiment, asking, "Why is it good to focus on the group, rather than myself? Why shouldn't I just do what makes me happy?"

When the hippies did commit to the bonds of family and community, they often did so only insofar as it remained pleasing to do so. An example can be found in the commune phenomenon of the late 1960s. Though thousands of hippies joined communes, only a few hundred remained for more than a few months, largely because

Consensual Crime

Hippies believed they should be allowed to do anything, even harmful things, so long as they were only harming themselves. Modern debates, such as the right to engage in same-sex marriage and the debate over physician-assisted suicide, were born from the hippie insistence on questioning society's restraints on consensual behavior.

functional communal life requires placing the needs of the group ahead of the desires of the individual.

In the end, the hip individualism can be summarized by saying that, while many hippies believed in community in principle, they had come to absorb the hippie mantra "if it feels good, do it" and, as it turned out, things like marriage, community involvement, and dedication to one's profession did not always feel good. A new mantra had been developed: "if it doesn't feel good, don't do it."

Of course, by rejecting the conventional roles ascribed to family and marriage, the hippies violated the "so long as no one gets hurt," part of their credo. Children who resulted from hippie unions were all too often the unfortunate casualties of the "I've only got one life and I'd better make it good" mentality.

For those whose commitment to the idea of alternative community was stronger than their desire for personal fulfillment, the rural commune proved the only tenable answer to the quest. Laws and conventional culture were too strong and too prevalent in urban environments and, more often than not, crushed the utopians into submission. Elements of hip culture survived in the cities, but only after they were altered to a form deemed more acceptable to the masses. In rural environments, like the badlands of South Dakota and the farmlands of Northern California, a few hippies persevered, creating sustainable, cooperative communities where the ideal hip life could flourish.

Those who were successful in the communal experiment were forced to find a balance between personal and group goals, more focused on individual happiness than the conformists of the 1940s and 1950s, but willing to recognize the need to subordinate for mutual benefit. It was perhaps *only* in the communes that the hip vision

A village hippie plows the soil while another plays music in the background. (© 2009 Robert Altman. Used by permission. Appears in Robert Altman, The Sixties *[Santa Monica Press, 2007].)*

found its most complete expression, communities tied to the meat of mainstream culture but still independent enough to allow a flowering of alternative lifestyles. The committed communards were, at the end of the era, the ones who kept the dream alive.

Ruminations

We have examined the legacy of the hippies through several facets: globalization, the formation of a new consumer culture, and the perspective on individualism versus community. This discussion only begins to address the effect that the hippies had on American and global culture. The hippies helped to advance the causes of women's liberation, civil rights, artistic expression, freedom of speech, freedom of the press, expansion of education, and antiwar/violence. They constitute one of the most important counterculture groups ever to emerge from American culture.

At the root of all these changes was a generation of people asking, "Why are things the way they are?" They asked the government to justify its policies, asked the people to justify their faith in their government, asked the church to justify the allegiance of the faithful, and asked themselves and each other, "How do we live the life we *want* to live, rather than the one we are *supposed* to live?" It was their willingness to question the status quo that gave the hippies such impact.

But it takes more than simply questioning the norm; to create change one must be willing to act. From setting up psychedelic shops on the streets of San Francisco and communes in the fields of Kansas, to marching on the streets of Chicago, the hippies were part of the ruminations that changed the country. From their desire to find happiness, fulfillment, community, individuality, expression, and love, they were determined to live life on their own terms.

The mainstream reacted with fear, chastising and dismissing the hippies as freaks and degenerates but, in secret, America's curiosity was piqued. Over the ensuing decades, as the hippies were repositioned within the American mosaic, the mainstream began to resemble the counterculture. It is partially because of the hippies that diversity has gained ground as an accepted recipe for success in all endeavors. Similarly, the audacity to question the status quo is increasingly considered central to the American way of life. In the 21st century, questioning the government, challenging oppression and discrimination, and upholding personal liberty are no longer the goals of the counterculture, they are part of the American code and the duty of every citizen. This is the hippies' legacy.

Notes

1. John Leland, *Hip: The History* (New York: HarperCollins, 2004), 4–10.
2. Craig Chalquist, *Deep California* (San Diego, CA: Craig Chalquist, 2008), 570–90.
3. Ronald E. Powaski, *Toward and Entangling Alliance* (Westport, CT: Greenwood Publishing Group, 1991), 216–23.
4. Michael Kort, *The Columbia Guide to the Cold War* (Irvington, NY: Columbia University Press, 2001), 3–15.
5. Stephen J. Whitfield, *The Culture of the Cold War*, 2nd ed. (Baltimore: Johns Hopkins University Press, 1996), 153–79.
6. Michael Curtain, "Dynasty in Drag," in *The Revolution Wasn't Televised*, ed. Lynn Spigel and Michael Curtain (New York: Routledge, 1997), 245–47.

7. Christopher Dunn, *Brutality Garden: Tropicalia and the Emergence of a Brazilian Counterculture* (Chapel Hill: University of North Carolina Press, 2001), 12–35.

8. David A. Fennell, *Ecotourism*, 2nd ed. (New York: Routledge, 2003), 17–30.

9. Bryan S. Turner, "Strategic Generations," in *Generational Consciousness, Narrative and Politics*, ed. June Edmunds and Bryan S. Turner (Lanham, MD: Rowman and Littlefield, 2003), 13–28.

10. Nadya Zimmerman, *Counterculture Kaleidoscope: Musical and Cultural Perspectives on Late Sixties San Francisco* (Ann Arbor: University of Michigan Press, 2008).

11. Marcel Danesi, *Why It Sells: Decoding the Meanings of Brand Names, Logos, Ads, and Other Marketing and Advertising Ploys* (Lanham, MD: Rowman and Littlefield, 2007), 160–80.

12. Geoffrey T. Holtz, *Welcome to the Jungle: The Why Behind Generation X* (New York: Macmillan, 1995), 51–80.

13. Tom Wolfe, "The 'Me' Decade and the Third Great Awakening," *New York* magazine, August 23, 1976.

14. Scott McFarlane, *The Hippie Narrative: A Literary Perspective on the Counterculture* (Jefferson, NC: McFarland Publications, 2007), 120–40.

15. Theodore Caplow et al., *The First Measured Century* (Washington, DC: American Enterprise Institute, 2001), 60–75.

Biographical Sketches

The Gurus

As the political and social environment drove the formation of sixties counterculture, a small number of leaders emerged, becoming teachers, mentors, and idols to the hippies. These leaders were sometimes called "gurus," a term borrowed from Hinduism and Tibetan Buddhism usually taken to mean "spiritual teacher."

The hippies generalized the meaning of the term, using it to refer to any leader with an important message to share, whether social, spiritual, or political. The gurus were the driving force in hippie life and demonstrated, for the hippies on the streets, the potential of the evolving counterculture worldview.

Richard "Baba Ram Dass" Alpert (1931–)

Dr. Richard Alpert, also known by his spiritual name Baba Ram Dass, was one of the premier social and spiritual leaders of the Haight-Ashbury hippies. Alpert took part in Timothy Leary's LSD experiments in the early 1960s, and later became a key representative of the neo-Indian spiritualist movement of the late 1960s and early 1970s.

Alpert was born in 1931 into a prominent Massachusetts family, the youngest child of prominent East Coast lawyer George Alpert, who served as a president of the New York, New Haven and Hartford Railroad and helped to found Brandeis University.[1] Richard Alpert achieved a doctorate in psychology from Stanford University in 1957 and in 1958 accepted a position teaching psychology in the Department of Social Relations at Harvard University.[2]

At Harvard Alpert began working with Timothy Leary, a scientist studying the effects of hallucinogenic compounds. While Alpert later said he had begun experimenting with marijuana at Stanford, it was Leary who introduced Alpert to hallucinogens.[3] Alpert was a subordinate in Leary's lab, but helped Leary to recruit students for his experiments and participated in taking hallucinogens with Leary and students in the group.[4]

Alpert was plagued with low self-esteem, believing himself to be inferior to his peers, and he also struggled with his homosexuality, which he felt was an aberrant psychological dysfunction. While Leary was convinced that LSD provided a "specific cure for homosexuality," the drug did not reduce Alpert's attraction to men.[5] In Alpert's opinion, taking LSD did, however, increase his confidence as an intellectual.

While Alpert was never as strong a proponent of hallucinogen therapy as Leary, he played an important role in the psychedelic revolution. In *The Future of Religion*, writers Rodney Stark and William Bainbridge say of Alpert and Leary's experimentation, "they began a kind of ideological war against their social scientist and medical colleagues over the very nature of reality."[6]

Both Leary and Alpert were dismissed from Harvard University in September of 1963 and Alpert was charged with associating inappropriately with and giving drugs to undergraduate students. Alpert accompanied Leary to Millbrook, New York, where they attempted to create the type of utopian society envisioned in Aldous Huxley's famous work *Island*. Hundreds of spiritual seekers, musicians, poets, and prominent intellectuals visited Millbrook to experience the unique experiment. During their stay in Millbrook, Leary and Alpert coauthored the book *The Psychedelic Experience*, an exploration of the spiritual use of hallucinogens modeled after the *Tibetan Book of the Dead*.

Leary and Alpert eventually drifted apart, as Leary's views on drug use and society became more radical and Alpert became fascinated with Eastern spirituality. In 1967 Alpert traveled to India to

---

New Age

The alternative spiritual movements of the 1960s were the forerunners of the "New Age" movement of subsequent decades. Now used to describe anything having to do with alternative health, wellness, spirituality, and philosophy, New Ageism devolved into a largely commercial pursuit, trivializing alternative spirituality by marketing it as a product to Western consumers.

---

seek spiritual enlightenment. At an ashram near the foothills of the Himalayas, Alpert met Baba Neem Karoli, also known as Maharaj-ji, who became his spiritual teacher ("baba") and gave him the spiritual name "Ram Dass," which literally translates as "servant of Rama."[7]

Alpert returned to the United States in 1969, as the excess that characterized the hippie era had given way to a new youth culture in which many were seeking spiritual guidance. Convinced that Eastern spirituality could be of enormous psychological benefit, Alpert himself became a "baba" and began lecturing and teaching meditation, yoga, and other forms of spiritual exercise.

Known for his association with Leary and psychedelic spirituality, Alpert was invited to all the major hippie events of the late 1960s and early 1970s. As Baba Ram Dass, his fame grew and he became one of the most prominent spiritual teachers in late hippie society.

In 1971 Alpert released his most famous work, *Be Here Now,* a combination of Hinduism, Buddhism, and psychedelic neospirituality. Three years later, he founded the Hanuman Foundation, a school for Hindu spirituality. The Hanuman Foundation gave rise to several side projects, including the Prison Ashram Project, an outreach organization intended to provide spiritual instruction to prison inmates. Alpert continued lecturing and teaching Eastern spirituality into the 21st century, despite suffering a stroke in 1997 that limited his ability to communicate.

The story of Alpert's transformation to Ram Dass was the subject of the 2002 film *Ram Dass Fierce Grace,* which was called one of the best nonfiction works of the year.[8]

Notes

1. Robert Greenfield, *Timothy Leary: A Biography* (New York: Harcourt Trade Publishers, 2006), 109.

2. Paul Harvey and Philip Goff, *The Columbia Documentary History of Religion in America since 1945: Religion in Cold War America* (New York: Columbia University Press, 2005), 95.

3. Greenfield, *Timothy Leary*, 108.

4. Ibid., 109.

5. Ibid., 289.

6. Rodney Stark and William Sims Bainbridge, *The Future of Religion: Secularization, Revival and Cult Formation* (Berkeley: University of California Press, 1986), 411.

7. Philip Lutgendorf, *Hanuman's Tale: The Message of a Divine Monkey* (New York: Oxford University Press, 2007), 271.

8. Thomas A. Forsthoefel and Cynthia Ann Humes, *Gurus in America* (Albany: SUNY Press, 2005).

Irwin Allen Ginsberg (1926–97)

For many hippies, poet Allen Ginsberg embodied the spirit of the generation. In his poetry, Ginsberg explored both the landscape of his own psyche, having struggled with his homosexuality and a difficult family life, and the political and social environment of the era. In the 1960s Ginsberg became a deep believer in the transformative power of psychedelic drugs and Eastern spiritual traditions, and became one of the most influential gurus and activists of the decade, serving as a reluctant leader to thousands of hippies who followed both his work and his actions with reverence.

Before he became a guru, Ginsberg was a Beat poet. The first reading of his most famous poem, *Howl*, to a group of fellow poets and Beat intellectuals at the Six Gallery in San Francisco in October of 1955 has been cited as the birth of the "San Francisco Poetry Renaissance."[1] As Ginsberg pored through the poem, railing against the "establishment" and expressing the anguish of a generation, members of the audience heard something special in his verse—the ruminations of a change that would transform the nature of art and culture.

Before he was a Beat poet, Ginsberg was a troubled child growing up in Newark, New Jersey. His mother, Naomi Ginsberg, was a major influence on his later work in two ways. First, she introduced him to the radical left of the 1950s, as she was a member of that era's communist movement. Second, his mother's struggle with mental illness, which culminated in a lobotomy, shock therapy, and confinement in a mental institution, was the source of much of the pain that Ginsberg scribbled into his poetry. He spent years in psychoanalysis attempting to come to grips with his past, including his mother's illness and his own homosexuality.[2]

Ginsberg attended Columbia University and learned from a number of esteemed poets, including Mark Van Doren and Raymond Weaver. It was there that Ginsberg met the members of his "inner circle," including Jack Kerouac and William S. Burroughs. Ginsberg also met his closest friend, and sometimes lover, Neal Cassady, a drifter who had traveled with Kerouac and was featured prominently in Kerouac's novel *On the Road*. Ginsberg, Cassady, Kerouac, and Burroughs were at the center of the Beat Generation and their writings and poetry formed the nucleus for the literary movement that described, informed, and inspired the phenomenon.[3]

In the early to mid-1950s, Ginsberg traveled to Mexico and began experimenting with psychedelic drugs. He eventually lived in San Francisco, where he had a relationship with fellow poet Peter Orlovsky. He and Orlovsky traveled around Africa, South America, Europe, and finally spent more than two years in India, where Ginsberg became deeply involved in meditation and Hinduism. Ginsberg returned to the United States in 1963, just as hippie culture was in the early stages of formation.

Ginsberg's poetry was already an inspiration for many hippie-era intellectuals and was seen as the benchmark for "stream of consciousness" writing. In the mid-1960s, Ginsberg became famous for his belief in Eastern spirituality and was an idol for thousands who had also turned to the East for enlightenment. He was a regular at hippie gatherings, where he would read poetry, lecture about philosophy and spirituality, and lead the crowds in Vedic chanting. Among hundreds of events, Ginsberg was a featured performer at the Human Be-In in 1967 and the Yip-Out at the 1968 Democratic National Convention.

As a writer, diplomat, and teacher, Ginsberg helped to bridge the gap between the countercultures of the Beats and the hippies. He remained active as a poet throughout the 1970s and 1980s and later in his life, he became an outspoken defender of free speech, even in controversial arenas. Ginsberg spent years traveling the college circuit, lecturing about spirituality, speech, and poetry.[4] Ginsberg died in 1997 of complications from liver cancer, leaving behind a body of work that cemented him as one of the most influential modern American writers.

Notes

1. Gerard DeGroot, *The Sixties Unplugged: A Kaleidoscopic History of a Disorderly Decade* (Cambridge, MA: Harvard University Press, 2008), 24–25.
2. Barry Miles, *Ginsberg: A Biography* (New York: Viking Press, 1989).
3. Jonah Raskin, *American Scream: Allen Ginsberg's Howl and the Making of the Beat Generation* (Berkeley: University of California Press, 2004).
4. Miles, *Ginsberg*, 272–300.

Elton "Ken" Kesey (1935–2001)

As a cult figure, author, and activist, Ken Kesey played a role in both the Beat Generation and the subsequent hippie era. A native of Colorado who spent much of his life in Eugene, Oregon, Kesey first took an interest in the counterculture after reading the works of Beat poets and novelists like Jack Kerouac and William Burroughs. Kesey first began writing in the late 1950s but it was not until the early 1960s that his novels gained national attention.

While his first novel, *Zoo*, which followed characters in the California Beat scene, was largely ignored, his second novel, *One Flew Over the Cuckoo's Nest*, which was released in 1962, became one of the most popular novels of the 1960s. The book was partially inspired by a brief period in 1959 when Kesey took LSD in a series of experiments conducted at Menlo Park Veterans' Hospital. The 1975 film adaptation of the book was a major critical hit and won five Academy Awards, though Kesey vocally criticized changes that were made to the novel in the transition. Following his experience at Menlo Park, Kesey took an active interest in hallucinogens. Kesey reported later that he often used LSD and other hallucinogens, like peyote, while writing.

While he began to gain notoriety as an author, his secondary career as the organizer of hallucinogenic parties also made Kesey a hippie icon. In 1964, when preparing for a promotional appearance after the publication of his third book, *Sometimes a Great Notion*, Kesey and several of his friends, who called themselves the "Merry Pranksters," decided to take a road trip. Over the next two years, the Pranksters toured the United States and Mexico, driving a converted school bus painted in psychedelic colors and mounted with a sign on the front that read "Furthur."[1] Along the way, Kesey and fellow Prankster Ken Babbs organized "acid tests," dance parties in which participants were given LSD, sometimes unknowingly, mixed into glasses of punch or Kool-aid. The Pranksters' trip from California to New York became the substrate for the 1968 Tom Wolfe novel *The Electric Kool-Aid Acid Test*.[2]

To Kesey, taking LSD and other psychedelics was a "test" of character and a chance to expand one's consciousness. While Kesey shared with Timothy Leary a deep belief in the transformative power of psychedelic drugs, he and Leary differed in their approaches. While Leary was deeply convinced that taking psychedelics should be a spiritual experience, Kesey was more interested in the revolutionary and recreational aspects. When he wasn't staging the parties, Kesey was often a guest, appearing at major gatherings and, occasionally, lecturing to the gathered crowds about alternative lifestyle, the ills of society, and the benefit of rebellion.

In 1965 Kesey took the lead in organizing a "truce" between the hippies and the Hells Angels. Before the truce, the militantly patriotic Angels would sometimes violently disrupt hippies' attempts to hold anti-Vietnam rallies and other antigovernment protests. Kesey decided to invite the Angels to an acid party and there he and friend Allen Ginsberg spoke to leading Angels, convincing them that the two groups should work together, as they shared a common, rebellious spirit. The Angels agreed and even helped Kesey stage several of his acid test parties. Kesey is credited with opening the lines of communication between the "freaks" and the Angels.[3]

Kesey was arrested in 1965 for possession of marijuana, and after an ill-conceived attempt to fake his own suicide and escape to Mexico he returned to the United States and spent five months in jail. Kesey continued traveling and staging hippie parties until late 1967 when he and his wife decided to retire to their farm in Pleasant Hill, Oregon. While Kesey continued to publish articles and books, none had the impact of his first two novels.[4] Kesey suffered a stroke in 1997 and never fully recovered. He died at his home in 2001, after several years of deteriorating health.

Notes

1. Steven Watson, *The Birth of the Beat Generation: Visionaries, Rebels, and Hipsters, 1944–1960* (New York: Pantheon Books, 1995), 280–90.

2. Paul Perry, et al., *On the Bus: The Complete Guide to the Legendary Trip of Ken Kesey and the Merry Pranksters and the Birth of the Counterculture* (New York: Thunder's Mouth Press, 1996).
3. Alice Echols, *Shaky Ground: The Sixties and Its Aftershocks* (New York: Columbia University Press, 2002), 43.
4. Stephen L. Tanner, *Ken Kesey* (New York: Twayne Publishers, 1984).

Timothy Francis Leary (1920–96)

Timothy Leary, born October 22, 1920, in Springfield, Massachusetts, was an experimental psychologist who became one of the most important social and cultural theorists of the hippie era. Though best known as a proponent of psychedelic drugs as an avenue for spiritual, cultural, and interpersonal enlightenment, Leary was a promoter of emerging ideas throughout his life.

The phrase "Turn on, tune in, drop out," which became a mantra for the hip generation, summarized Leary's philosophy during the height of his influence. Leary first uttered those words during a mass lecture to the hundreds assembled at the 1967 Human Be-In in San Francisco's Golden Gate Park. He explained the idea in his book of the same name:

> Drop Out—detach yourself from social drama, which is as dehydrated and ersatz as TV. Turn On—find a sacrament that returns you to the temple of God, your own body. Go out of your mind. Get high. Tune In—be reborn. Drop back in to express it. Start a new sequence of behavior that reflects your vision.[1]

Leary earned a Ph.D. in psychology from the University of California at Berkeley in 1950 and started his career in Oakland, California. Events in Leary's life, including the suicide of his wife in 1955, may have predisposed him to develop a rebellious attitude toward conventional therapy and contributed to his willingness to explore alternative treatments. Along with friend and colleague Dr. Richard Alpert, Leary began experimenting with psychoactive substances, including hallucinogenic mushrooms, mescaline, peyote, and LSD.[2]

From 1959 to 1963 Leary worked at Harvard University, where he experimented with using hallucinogens to treat a variety of psychological ailments. During this time, he became convinced that

Timothy Leary in Berkeley, California, 1969. (© 2009 Robert Altman. Used by permission. Appears in Robert Altman, The Sixties *[Santa Monica Press, 2007].)*

hallucinogenic compounds held the key to spiritual and personal enlightenment. In 1963 Leary and Alpert were dismissed from Harvard for giving hallucinogens to undergraduate students, after which they began using the home of a friend, in Millbrook, New York, as the headquarters for their experiments.[3]

At Millbrook Leary created an experimental communal society where drugs, sex, and other forms of alternative social contact were used to broaden the horizons. To give credence to his research, Leary founded a spiritual society called the League for Spiritual Discovery (LSD), which became one of the best-known "psychedelic churches" of the era.[4]

Leary also spread his teachings through books and articles. His best-known works include *The Politics of Ecstasy* (1968), which discusses the social and spiritual uses of psychedelic drugs, and *High Priest* (1968), which discusses the relationship between culture and mysticism.

While Leary was not alone in using hallucinogens and other drugs in a search for personal development, his prominence made him a prime enemy of those opposed to hippie culture. Leary was arrested for the first time in 1965 for possession of marijuana, while crossing the border from Mexico. After racking up a list of small charges, he was arrested again in 1969 and sentenced to 10 to 30 years in prison.

Leary was imprisoned at the California Men's Colony at San Luis Obispo, but escaped with the help of sympathetic supporters and, allegedly, a group of prominent drug dealers, who paid members of the activist organization Weather Underground to help Leary. He escaped by climbing up a telephone pole and across a cable over the wall of the prison. Leary first fled to Algeria, where he stayed with exiled revolutionary and former Black Panther Eldridge Cleaver. He then stayed in Switzerland before deciding in 1973 to move to Afghanistan, a country with no extradition treaty. Leary was arrested at the airport in Kabul, Afghanistan, before he could exit the plane, thereby circumventing the extradition treaty requirements.[5] Leary was sentenced to 95 years in prison but was released in 1976, less than three years later, after he agreed to provide information to federal authorities in return for a reduced sentence.

Until his death in 1996 Leary continued writing and lecturing, turning from psychedelic spirituality to cybernetics. In Leary's opinion, freedom of information and global connectivity had the potential for the same consciousness-expanding enlightenment that he attributed to psychedelic drugs.[6] In the re-publication of his seminal work

The Politics of Ecstasy, in 1998, Leary's updated foreword clearly indicated that, while the content of his lectures had changed, his revolutionary spirit endured:

> In the cybernetic Twenty-First Century power will come, not from the barrel of a gun, but from the minds of free individuals using camera lenses, computer screens, and electronic networks. Question authority and just say "Know"![7]

Notes

1. Timothy Leary, *Turn On, Tune In, Drop Out* (Berkeley, CA: Ronin Publishers, 1999), 3.
2. Robert Greenfield, *Timothy Leary: A Biography* (New York: Harcourt Trade Publishers, 2006), 80–90.
3. William Lawlor, *Beat Culture: Lifestyle, Icons and Impact* (Oxford: ABC-Clio Press, 2005), 201.
4. Martin Torgoff, *Can't Find My Way Home: America in the Great Stoned Age, 1945–2000* (New York: Simon and Schuster, 2004), 200–210.
5. Greenfield, *Timothy Leary*, 380–90, 515–18.
6. "Timothy Leary," *The Economist*, June 1996, 1.
7. Timothy Leary, *The Politics of Ecstasy*, 2nd ed. (Berkeley, CA: Ronin Publishing, 1998), 10.

The Artists

The art and music of the hippie era was the lifeblood of the counterculture and in the decades that followed would serve as a lasting record of the counterculture, preserving the spirit of rebellion and freedom that gave way to the hippie phenomenon.

Joan Chandos Baez (1941–)

Joan Baez is one of the few musicians whose political activities rival her musical impact. Over the course of her career, Baez has earned six gold records and four Grammy Award nominations. Her music explores deep political themes including the civil rights movement, antiwar politics, and environmental preservation. Baez has also appeared at hundreds of marches, rallies, and demonstrations from the 1960s into the 21st century.[1]

Baez was born in 1941 in Staten Island, New York, and raised, with her two sisters, in a modest Quaker family. Baez's father worked for the United Nations Educational, Scientific, and Cultural Organization (UNESCO) and, as a result, the family moved frequently, leading Baez to spend portions of her childhood in the Middle East and Europe. Baez later claimed that her early travels informed her views on global politics, while her family's spiritual beliefs laid the foundation for her own belief in the philosophy of nonviolence, to which she would later add inspiration from Eastern spirituality.

In 1956 Baez attended a speech by civil rights leader Martin Luther King Jr., who later became one of her close friends. In her memoirs Baez listed her first meeting with King as a formative event in her life. When she began writing songs that same year, Baez almost immediately opted for deep political themes, though she also imitated folk artists like Pete Seeger, whom she saw in concert in 1957.[2]

After moving with her family to Belmont, Massachusetts, in 1958, Baez became a regular of the coffeehouse performance scene in Cambridge. She gave her first concert at "Club 47," a music venue located at 47 Mount Auburn Street in Cambridge, and from there her career quickly expanded. By 1960 Baez was one of the premier artists in the folk revival movement, which saw artists reviving songs from the past that shared a thematic thread—exploring the injustices of everyday life and society. While the movement began by reviving Appalachian folk music and Negro spirituals, innovators like Baez soon began writing folk songs about modern issues.

Baez met Bob Dylan in 1961 in Greenwich Village, New York, and took an immediate liking to the innovative young musician. Baez became Dylan's patron, bringing him to her concerts and promoting his music, despite the fact that he was initially unpopular with audiences. By that time, Baez had already released her first album and her popularity was growing. Their friendship became a romance that lasted through 1965, during which time Baez credits Dylan with helping her to develop her own unique sound.[3]

Baez participated in Martin Luther King Jr.'s march on Birmingham, Alabama, in 1963, as well as his march on Washington, DC, later that year. Her performance of the protest song "We Shall Overcome," though originally popularized by Pete Seeger, permanently linked her to the song and she recorded it on a subsequent album. Baez's involvement in civil rights marches continued throughout the

1960s and she appeared at a number of prominent anti-Vietnam protests. On August 13, 1967, Baez was banned from performing at the Washington Monument, after the Daughters of the American Revolution protested her vocal opposition to the Vietnam War.

Though her popularity peaked in the mid-1960s as electric rock consumed the American consciousness, Baez has continued performing into the 21st century and remains deeply involved in politics. Speaking about Baez's popularity in the folk revival, writer Avital H. Bloch said in her 2005 book *Impossible to Hold*, "Her singing seemed to provide a political message about roots, equality, and simplicity that meshed with the emerging new left's protest against middle-class values, an alienating urban environment, the toughness of the Cold War, and an unresponsive political system."[4]

Notes

1. Charles J. Fuss, *Joan Baez: A Bio-Bibliography* (Westport, CT: Greenwood Press, 1996).
2. Avital H. Bloch and Lauri Umansky, *Impossible to Hold: Women and Culture in the 1960s* (New York: NYU Press, 2005), 127.
3. Jerome L. Rodnitzky, *Feminist Phoenix: The Rise and Fall of a Feminist Counterculture* (Westport, CT: Praeger Publishers, 1999).
4. Bloch, *Impossible to Hold*, 129.

Jerome "Jerry" Garcia (1942–95)

Jerry Garcia was the lead singer and songwriter for the Grateful Dead, one of the most influential and enduring psychedelic rock bands to emerge from the San Francisco hippie scene. Garcia was a founding member of the group, which evolved from a blues-rock act known as the Warlocks, and he remained with "the Dead," as they were widely known, touring and recording until his death in 1995 from a heart attack.

Garcia was born August 1, 1942, in San Francisco, California. He was introduced to music at a young age, studying piano and later guitar. In 1960, at age 17, Garcia ran away from home to join the Army, and spent seven months in Fort Ord in Monterey Bay, California. Garcia was a poor and disinterested recruit and was dismissed in December of 1960, having accrued a large number of citations and AWOL reports.

Jerry Garcia in the Golden Gate Park Panhandle, 1968. (© 2009 Robert Altman. Used by permission. Appears in Robert Altman, The Sixties *[Santa Monica Press, 2007].)*

Homeless and without direction, Garcia spent several years moving around the San Francisco area. He experimented with drugs and was inspired by the literature and music of the Beat Generation. Garcia had been playing guitar privately, but considered it a hobby, believing that he would pursue painting as a profession. Garcia married his first wife, Sarah Ruppenthal, in 1963 and the couple had their first daughter in December of that same year.[1]

By 1962 Garcia was performing bluegrass and old-time standards with friends he met in San Francisco. Garcia was one of the innovators of the San Francisco scene, borrowing from a variety of genres to carve out a unique musical niche. Garcia often used a "call and response" system, common in bluegrass and jazz music, which allowed for improvisation and immediacy. Biographer Blair Jackson would say of Garcia in his 2000 biography, *Garcia*, "No modern popular musician ever worked so deeply in so many different styles as Garcia did."[2]

In the mid-1960s, Garcia began experimenting with LSD and became associated with the cult figures of the era, including Ken Kesey, Neal Cassady, and their road-tripping companions, the Merry Pranksters. Through Kesey and Cassady, Garcia met Carolyn "Mountain Girl" Adams, with whom he had two children. The couple married in 1981.

Garcia and most of the musicians who would later form the Dead performed their first concert together in 1964, under the name the Warlocks. Soon after, the band chose the name "the Grateful Dead," which Garcia claimed was chosen by opening the dictionary at random before a show. The name was a term for an angel who feels a sense of gratitude for the person who arranged his or her burial. Though the name was intended as a temporary choice, after graphic artists Alton Kelley and Stanley "Mouse" Miller designed the band's famous "skull and roses" logo, Garcia and his friends decided the name would stay.[3]

The Grateful Dead was one of the headlining bands at the 1967 Human Be-In in Golden Gate Park and would thereafter remain one of the most popular hippie-era rock bands. That year, Mickey Hart and Tom Constanten joined the group and their style evolved further toward the experimental psychedelic sound. Over decades of touring, the Grateful Dead's concerts became a cult tradition, attracting new generations of counterculture aficionados to their shows, alongside throngs of old fans.

Garcia and the Dead continued playing together until shortly before Garcia's death in 1995. Over the years, Garcia was also involved in a number of other projects, including touring and recording solo or with other musicians as the Jerry Garcia Band. Garcia

---

Deadheads

The Grateful Dead toured continuously from 1965 until the death of front man Jerry Garcia in 1995 and, during that time, developed a cult following to rival any trend in American history. The band's fans, often called "Deadheads," included thousands of touring hippies who would follow the band from venue to venue throughout the year.

---

performed and recorded with a number of prominent musicians, including Bob Dylan and David Grisman.

Though Garcia remained married to Adams until 1994, their relationship deteriorated in the 1980s, as Garcia would often leave home for long periods and was known to carry on romantic relationships with other women. In 1986 Garcia went into a diabetic coma and spent months in recovery. He eventually returned to touring, but drug and alcohol abuse constantly resurfaced in his life and ultimately led to his death.[4]

Notes

1. Robert Greenfield, *Dark Star: An Oral Biography of Jerry Garcia* (New York: William Morrow, 1996).
2. Blair Jackson, *Garcia: An American Life* (New York: Penguin, 2000), xi.
3. Ibid., 85.
4. Greenfield, *Dark Star*.

Chester Leo "Chet" Helms (1942–2005)

Music promoter and party organizer Chet Helms was a major figure in the San Francisco music scene of the 1960s. He is often credited with being the first promoter to produce psychedelic rock concerts in San Francisco, and is therefore considered an important figure in the evolution of American music.

Helms was born in Santa Maria, California, to a middle-class Baptist family. He spent most of his youth in Missouri and Texas, where he became fascinated with the writings and lifestyle of the Beat

Generation. Helms attended the University of Texas and was involved in the music scene there, promoting local singers and organizing concerts. Helms also began using drugs while at the university and his increasing reliance on drugs contributed to his decision to drop out. After spending a year traveling, Helms settled in San Francisco.

When he arrived in San Francisco in 1962, Helms found a vibrant music scene with little direction and/or leadership. He stayed at boarding houses in Haight-Ashbury, especially 1090 Page Street, which became a popular spot for parties. Helms helped to organize a Wednesday night jam session in the ballroom-sized basement of the Page Street flophouse.[1]

By 1965 Helms was also working with the Family Dog, a community of hippies living in a house at 2125 Pine Street. Helms became close with many of the hippies living at the Pine Street house and, in February of that year, he decided to form "Family Dog Promotions," working with several other members of the commune to produce concerts at the Fillmore Auditorium.

At the Fillmore, Helms competed with rival promoter Bill Graham, who took a vastly different approach to the music business. While Graham was a businessman who demanded strict adherence to contracts and paid close attention to profit margins, Helms was part of the hippie community and operated his "business" in accordance with the principles of that society. Helms didn't rely on contracts and he was loose regarding payment. Graham eventually convinced management at the Fillmore that he would bring in a more reliable profit, and Helms switched venues to the Avalon Ballroom. Shortly thereafter, Helms expanded his operations and began promoting shows at Longshoremen's Hall.[2]

In 1966 Helms convinced Janis Joplin, a friend he met while living in Texas, to join a new band, Big Brother and the Holding Company, which Helms had just agreed to manage. It wasn't long before Joplin became one of the rising queens of psychedelic rock, thanks in part to Helms's shrewd vision.

In a 2005 article in the *San Francisco Chronicle*, published shortly after Helms's death, drummer Mickey Hart of the Grateful Dead said of him, "He was really the heart and soul of the music scene here in San Francisco. He was more than just a promoter. The Avalon really captured the spirit and the vibe of the era."[3]

Chet Helms, hippie promoter. (© 2009 Robert Altman. Used by permission. Appears in Robert Altman, The Sixties *[Santa Monica Press, 2007].)*

Helms retired from full-time promotion in the 1970s, but occasionally resurfaced to produce concerts in San Francisco, including a 1997 concert to celebrate the 30th anniversary of the Summer of Love. Helms died in 2005 of complications from a stroke, after suffering for years from hepatitis C. In October of 2005, San Francisco celebrated Helms's life with a free concert called the "Tribal Stomp" in Golden Gate Park.

"He wasn't just a promoter; he was a supporter of music and art," said Barry Melton, lead guitarist for Country Joe and the Fish. "He supported people emotionally, psychologically, and psychically. He really made the scene what it was."[4]

Notes

1. Gene Anthony, *Summer of Love: Haight Ashbury at Its Finest* (Bloomington, IN: John Libbey Publishers, 1995), 48–51.
2. Barry Miles, *Hippie* (New York: Sterling Publishing Co., 2004), 100.
3. Aidin Vaziri and Jim Herron Zamora, "Chet Helms—Legendary S.F. Rock Music Producer," *San Francisco Chronicle*, June 26, 2005.
4. Ibid., 1–2.

James Marshall "Jimi" Hendrix (1942–70)

Jimi Hendrix remains one of the most celebrated guitarists, songwriters, and musicians in the history of American rock. Hendrix first achieved fame in the United Kingdom, before exploding onto the U.S. scene with a breakthrough performance at the 1967 Monterey Pop Festival. Hendrix was an international success and a rising star until his untimely death in 1970 from a drug overdose.

Hendrix was born in 1942 in Seattle, Washington, into a family afflicted by poverty and instability. His mother named him "Johnny Allen Hendrix" but his father later changed his name to "James Marshall" in memoriam of the child's deceased uncle. Three of Hendrix's four siblings were born with developmental disabilities and all of the Hendrix children, including Jimi, were committed to state care because of the family's financial destitution. Hendrix's parents divorced when he was 9 and his mother died shortly before he turned 15.

Hendrix took an early interest in music, having grown up listening to his father's R&B records. In biographical accounts, it is often reported that Hendrix imitated playing guitar on a broom before he was given his first instrument, a ukulele, around his 15th birthday. Later, Hendrix's father gave him an acoustic guitar and Hendrix learned to play by imitating his idols. Though he was left-handed,

Hendrix played a right-handed guitar upside down. Though guitar makers produce left-handed instruments, Hendrix maintained his upside-down style, giving him a unique approach to chord voicings and melodic arrangement.

Hendrix spent his teenage years playing with local Seattle bands, including a band called the Velvetones, which performed covers of R&B hits. In 1960 Hendrix was arrested for riding in a stolen car, his second arrest of that nature, and was given a choice between the military and prison. Hendrix enlisted in May of 1961 and spent three years with the Army.[1]

From 1963 to 1966 Hendrix traveled the United States and built a successful career as a backing musician. Living in Tennessee and later New York City, Hendrix played for, among a host of other musicians, Sam Cooke, the Isley Brothers, Ike and Tina Turner, and Little Richard. Hendrix lived for a time in Harlem, New York, but soon preferred to spend his time on the Lower East Side, where East Coast hippie culture was beginning to spread and where the fans shared Hendrix's tastes in fashion and recreational drugs.[2]

It was through a 1966 meeting with Linda Keith, then girlfriend of Rolling Stone's guitarist Keith Richards, that Hendrix met Chas Chandler, a former bassist for the the Animals, who was seeking to become a promoter. Chandler was enamored by Hendrix's version of the song "Hey Joe," and flew him to London where he helped Hendrix form "The Jimi Hendrix Experience."

With bassist Noel Redding and drummer Mitch Mitchell, the Experience became a major success in bohemian London. As there was no R&B scene in London, Hendrix, Redding, and Mitchell blended R&B structures and lyrics with the emerging psychedelic rock sound. The effect was instantaneously recognizable to thousands of fans as something innovative and new. The band's first album, *Are You Experienced*, was released in May of 1967, and quickly hit number 2 on the UK pop charts.[3]

In June of 1967 Jimi Hendrix played at the Monterey International Pop Festival, the concert that introduced psychedelic rock to mainstream American audiences. Hendrix's performance at Monterey is regarded by some critics as one of the best moments in U.S. music history.[4]

Now a major international success, Hendrix performed both in the United States and in London. His two subsequent releases with the Experience, *Axis: Bold as Love* and *Electric Ladyland,* were top-selling albums. While his guitar playing was the hook that grabbed many of his fans, Hendrix was also consistently praised for his lyricism, writing songs about counterculture ideals, racism, and social struggles. Struggles between Hendrix and Redding for control of the band brought an end to the Experience in 1968, but Hendrix continued playing, building a group of musicians who performed with him at various concerts.

Hendrix had begun using heroin and other drugs in the mid-1960s. By the time the Woodstock concert came about on August 18, 1969, Hendrix had formed a new band, which he called Gypsy Sun and Rainbows. Because of his popularity, Hendrix's band was asked to headline the concert. Despite difficulties that included a dwindling audience and poor sound engineering, Hendrix played a two-hour set that is considered one of the greatest performances of the concert, and which contained his now-famous version of "The Star Spangled Banner" on solo guitar, a recording that has become emblematic of the 1960s.[5]

Hendrix died in his sleep in September 1970, having aspirated his own vomit after ingesting a deadly mixture of liquor, drugs, and sleeping pills. Though his career was short, Hendrix's legacy endures because of his charisma as an artist and his continent-spanning popularity. Hendrix was one of only a few African Americans to make a lasting mark on the psychedelic rock scene, and therefore serves as a benchmark in African American culture as well. For decades after his death, guitarists and singers would continue to imitate Hendrix's unique and unusual sound.

Notes

1. Sharon Lawrence, *Jimi Hendrix: The Man, the Magic, the Truth* (New York: HarperCollins, 2005).
2. Charles R. Cross, *Room Full of Mirrors: A Biography of Jimi Hendrix* (New York: Hyperion Books, 2006).
3. Barry Miles, *Hippie* (New York: Sterling Publishing, 2004), 17.
4. Steven Roby, *Black Gold: The Lost Archives of Jimi Hendrix* (New York: Watson-Guptill Publications, 2002), 244.
5. Harry Shapiro and Caesar Glebbeek, *Jimi Hendrix: Electric Gypsy* (New York: Heinemann, 1990).

Janis Lyn Joplin (1943–70)

Singer/songwriter Janis Joplin is credited by many as the first female rock superstar.[1] Within three years of her start in the underground rock scene of San Francisco's Haight-Ashbury, Joplin became one of the most popular performers and recording artists in the country.

Joplin was born in 1943 in Port Arthur, Texas, into a middle-class family. Biographical sketches describe Joplin as something of a social outcast who chose to associate with others who were outside mainstream youth culture.[2] She took an early interest in music, especially classic blues, and was inspired by artists like Bessie Smith and Huddie "Leadbelly" Ledbetter.[3]

In 1963 Joplin traveled to San Francisco with friend and music promoter Chet Helms and spent much of 1963 and 1964 with a group of hippies and musicians in a boarding house at 1090 Page Street in Haight-Ashbury. Joplin took part-time gigs singing with various Bay Area groups and was soon using a variety of drugs, from marijuana to heroin.

In 1964 Joplin's friends convinced her to return to Port Arthur, realizing that her drug use had become life-threatening. For nearly a year Joplin managed to abstain from drugs and returned to school, while she continued performing as a solo act in nearby Austin. In 1966 Chet Helms asked Joplin to return to San Francisco to head a relatively unknown psychedelic rock band he was promoting called Big Brother and the Holding Company. Joplin agreed and joined the band in June of 1966, giving her first concert at the now-famous Avalon Ballroom.[4]

Joplin and Big Brother became a hit in the Haight, but were still unknown to the rest of the world. This would change in June of 1967, when they performed at the Monterey Pop Festival. Along with Jimi Hendrix, Jefferson Airplane, and a host of other Bay Area psychedelic rock bands, the pop festival was the largest commercial venue for the new sound and brought the Haight scene to the rest of the world.

All the bands at Monterey were asked to perform for free and to allow their performances to be filmed for a planned documentary. Helms and Big Brother refused to be included in the documentary because they were not being compensated. As a result, Joplin's performance at Monterey, heralded as one of the greatest rock performances of all time, was not recorded. The promoters asked her to return for a second performance, which she did, and two songs, a version of "Ball and Chain," and the song "Combination of the Two," were recorded. Many music critics refer to Joplin's first performance at Monterey as her "lost masterpiece."[5]

Joplin and Big Brother released their self-titled debut album in 1967, and in 1968 went on an East Coast tour that included a concert in New York City at Martin Luther King Jr.'s wake. In the spring of 1968 Joplin and Big Brother made their television debut on the *Dick Cavett Show*. In December 1968 Joplin left Big Brother and formed the Kozmic Blues Band, a new backing outfit with a more blues-oriented sound.[6]

While Joplin's concerts were a major draw, she was inconsistent as a performer due to heavy drug use. Joplin gave a disappointing concert at Woodstock in August of 1969, largely because she became drunk during her 10-hour wait for her time slot.[7] The Kozmic Blues Band broke up shortly thereafter and Joplin formed the Full Tilt Boogie Band, with whom she performed and recorded in the summer of 1970.

Joplin's personal life was as tumultuous as her on-stage persona. Known for her bisexuality and passionate, fiery romances, on the night of her death Joplin was reportedly expecting to meet with two lovers, Peggy Caserta and a young man named Seth Morgan, for group sex. Both lovers canceled and Joplin decided to shoot heroin by herself, unaware that the supply she had purchased was improperly cut and eight times stronger than the usual variety. Joplin died from an overdose and was found 18 hours later in her hotel room.

In 1971 the posthumous album *Pearl* was released, which contains many of Joplin's most famous songs, including "Me and Bobby McGee" and "Summertime." Joplin was inducted into the Rock and Roll Hall of Fame in 1995 and has been regularly listed by music critics as one of the top rock artists of all time.[8] While some critics dismiss Joplin as an imitator of African American singers, others believe that she created a new style, in the grey area between rock and blues. Legendary singer Etta James called Joplin "an angel who came and paved a road white chicks hadn't walked before."[9]

Notes

1. Scott Stanton, *The Tombstone Tourist: Musicians* (New York: Simon and Schuster, 2003), 138.
2. Alice Echols, *Scars of Sweet Paradise: The Life and Times and Janis Joplin* (New York: Henry Holt, 1999).
3. Gary Donaldson, *Modern America: A Documentary History of the Nation Since 1945* (Armonk, NY: M. E. Sharpe Publishers, 2007), 139.
4. Echols, *Scars of Sweet Paradise*.
5. Barry Miles, *Hippie* (New York: Sterling Publishing, 2004), 212.
6. Joplin, Laura, *Love, Janis* (New York: Villard Books, 1992).
7. Miles, *Hippie*, 319.
8. David Dalton, *Piece of My Heart: A Portrait of Janis Joplin* (New York: Da Capo Press, 1991).
9. Miles, *Hippie*, 304.

Stanley "Mouse" Miller (1940–)

While many hippies might not have known him by name, Stanley "Mouse" Miller's art was immediately recognizable to anyone in the 1960s in-crowd. An illustrator and graphic artist, Miller was one of the five most prominent psychedelic poster artists in the San Francisco hippie scene. Among his hundreds of album covers and promotional posters, Miller created logos and posters for Bob Dylan, Jerry Garcia, the Steve Miller Band, and Big Brother and the Holding Company.

Miller was born in California, but grew up in Detroit, Michigan, where his father worked as a cartoonist for Walt Disney.[1] Miller followed in his father's footsteps and began drawing cartoons at a young age. He was given the nickname "Mouse" in elementary school because he would always include a small cartoon rodent as a signature on his drawings.

Miller was expelled from high school for vandalism when it was discovered that he had decorated the walls of a popular teen hangout with his art. Miller then entered Detroit's underground hot-rod racing scene, a proving ground for a number of future graphic artists, including another of the big five poster artists, Rick Griffin. Miller got his start printing t-shirts and was soon asked to paint hot-rods.[2]

Miller relocated to San Francisco in 1965, as the hippie movement was kicking into high gear. There he met artist Alton Kelley, who had also cut his teeth in the underground hot-rod community and had been part of the "Red Dog Saloon Gang," one of the first hippie commune/concert halls.[3]

Miller and Kelley became fast friends and together joined the Family Dog, a group of hippies who promoted concerts in San Francisco, most famously at the Avalon Ballroom, Fillmore Auditorium, and Longshoremen's Hall. Chet Helms, then music promoter for the Family Dog, asked Miller and Kelley to design posters for upcoming shows.

Miller and Kelley set about educating themselves on poster design. They were especially attracted to art nouveau posters, which contained elements that seemed harmonious with the Victorian architecture of the Haight district.[4] "Stanley and I had no idea what we were doing," Kelley said in a 2007 interview for the *San Francisco Chronicle*, "but we went ahead and looked at American Indian stuff, Chinese stuff, Art Nouveau, Art Deco, Modern, Bauhaus, whatever."[5]

From 1965 to 1968 Miller and Kelley defined psychedelic art, and their posters were ubiquitous in the San Francisco hippie scene. One of Miller and Kelley's most famous posters became an advertisement for Zig-Zag, a brand of rolling papers popular with marijuana enthusiasts. The poster featured a stylized figure, looking vaguely Middle Eastern in reference to the origin of the company's tobacco, framed in a decorative art nouveau border. Miller and Kelley also began producing posters and album covers for some of the biggest musical acts on the West Coast, including the Grateful Dead and Janis Joplin.

After 1968 Chet Helms and other promoters started opting for different poster artists. Miller's fame waned and he left San Francisco, traveling abroad and then around the country. Kelley and Miller decided to work together again in 1971, and began producing album art and other promotional materials for rock bands. Some of the logos they created, both during their first peak and later during their revival, became iconic symbols, including the "skulls and roses" logo for the Grateful Dead and the "Pegasus" logo for the Steve Miller band.

From his home in Sonoma County, Miller continued working for bands and expanded his repertoire into fine arts. In 1993 doctors informed Miller that he would need a liver transplant, an operation that cost upwards of $500,000. The Grateful Dead and several other bands contributed funds to pay for Miller's operation and he eventually returned to his art.[6] In *The American Counterculture*, author Christopher Gair claims that Miller was significant not only for his art but for his unusual approach to art. "In some ways, his compositional style is reminiscent of Kerouac or of bebop musicians in that it is based on rapid, improvised sketching that draws on years of dedication to his craft."[7]

Notes

1. Christopher Gair, *The American Counterculture* (Edinburgh: Edinburgh University Press, 2007), 189.
2. Gayle Lemke, Jacaeber Kastor, and Mickey Hart, *The Art of the Fillmore* (New York: Thunder's Mouth Press, 2005), 91.
3. Alton Kelley, "Summer of Love: 40 Years Later," *San Francisco Chronicle*, May 20, 2007, 1.
4. Christoph Grunenberg and Jonathan Harris, *Summer of Love: Psychedelic Art, Social Crisis and Counterculture in the 1960s* (Liverpool: Liverpool University Press, 2005), 330.
5. Kelley, "Summer of Love," 2.
6. Steven Cerio, "Stanley Mouse," www.happyhomeland.com.
7. Gair, *American Counterculture*, 189.

Grace Slick (1939–)

Famed rocker Grace Slick, who became one of the biggest names in psychedelic rock, was born Grace Barnett Wing in 1939 in Highland Park, Illinois, a residential suburb near Chicago. Her family moved frequently when she was young and she spent much of her childhood in Palo Alto, California. According to her own description, Slick was experimenting with alcohol at a young age, and by 16 was already drawn to California's underground drug culture.

Slick married her first husband, cinematographer Gerald "Jerry" Slick, in 1961 and remained with him until 1971, though their relationship waned in the mid-1960s and Slick engaged in a number of short-term affairs.[1] In 1965 Slick, her husband, and several of their friends formed "The Great Society," an experimental psychedelic rock band that blended elements of rock, jazz, and blues.

The Great Society became an underground success in the Haight and Slick was undeniably the star of the show. The band began to disintegrate due to disagreements among the members and, in 1966 Marty Balin and Bill Thompson of the rock group Jefferson Airplane asked Slick to join the band. Slick made her first performance with Jefferson Airplane, replacing former singer Signe Anderson, at the Fillmore Auditorium in October of 1966.

Slick's songs "Somebody to Love" and "White Rabbit," which she wrote while with The Great Society, became the major hits from Jefferson Airplane's most popular album *Surrealistic Pillow*, released in 1967. Alongside fellow female singer Janis Joplin, Slick can be recognized as one of the first female rock stars. She was a major player in the San Francisco rock scene and formed close friendships with Joplin and Jerry Garcia of the Grateful Dead. In her memoirs, Slick described the era as one of "fun, drugs, and experimentation." Slick even claims to have had a short sexual relationship with Jim Morrison before his death.[2]

In an interview with *Life* magazine in December of 1992, Slick describes the way that drugs fueled the music of the era: "psychedelics were it—mushrooms, acid, marijuana. For the generation of the 60s, they were thought of as opening up a new way of seeing. You got a glimpse of other ways of interpreting, of communicating. It was very powerful. And there's no question that it affected our performances."[3]

Jefferson Airplane remained together until 1973 with Slick as the band's lead singer. After the group's decline, Slick and some remaining members of Jefferson Airplane formed Jefferson Starship. Slick also recorded and released solo work during this period. She left Jefferson Starship in 1978 and later helped form another offshoot of the original, called "Starship," which continued touring until 1988. Following Starship's breakup, Slick concentrated on nonmusical activities, including becoming a respected figure in the California fine arts community.

Notes

1. Jeff Tamarkin, Jann Wenner, and Paul Kantner, *Got a Revolution: The Turbulent Flight of Jefferson Airplane* (New York: Simon and Schuster, 2003), 102.
2. Grace Slick and Andrea Cagan, *Somebody to Love? A Rock-And-Roll Memoir* (Topeka, KS: Tandem Library, 1999).
3. "A Session with Grace Slick," *Live Magazine*, Special Issue: "40 Years of Rock 'n' Roll" (December 1, 1992).

James Vernon Taylor (1948–)

James Taylor epitomized the singer/songwriter movement of the 1970s, as the passionate fury of the "love decade" gave way to what writer Tom Wolfe called the "'Me' decade."[1] Taylor's sensitive ballads, while sharply contrasting with the energetic rhythms of 1960s rock, reflected the softer side of hippie culture and, more important, what hippies were in the process of becoming.

Taylor was born March 12, 1948, into a wealthy Boston family. He was introduced to music at a young age, learning cello and later guitar.[2] Taylor listened to rock, blues, folk, and country music and from these developed a unique style with tender lyricism, humor, and simple, sparse instrumentation. Taylor's family eventually moved to Chapel Hill, North Carolina, where Taylor played concerts at small venues.

In his teenage years Taylor was plagued by depression and prone to alcohol and drug abuse. Taylor committed himself to McLean Psychiatric Hospital in Belmont, Massachusetts, in 1965 for 10 months in an effort to fight his depression and drug use. After emerging he moved to New York to pursue his music, but soon developed a heroin habit that would stay with him for more than a decade. Taylor later said that it was his father's intervention, driving to New York City and bringing him back to North Carolina, that saved him from death.[3]

Taylor partially recovered but was still using drugs after returning to North Carolina. In 1967 Peter Asher, a former British invasion singer turned A&R representative for the Beatles' record label Apple Records, heard Taylor's music and asked him to come to England to record. Taylor spent much of 1968 recording material for what would become his first album, *James Taylor*.[4]

While Asher was convinced that Taylor could be a success, problems within the Beatles and Apple Records management, coupled with Taylor's struggles with drugs, prevented an effective promotion. Taylor underwent drug rehabilitation again in 1969, but then suffered a motorcycle accident that postponed his touring schedule.[5]

In 1969 Asher brought Taylor to Laurel Canyon, a part of Los Angeles that, over the next several years, became the soft-rock capital of the country. There Taylor met Carole King, Joni Mitchell, Jackson Browne, and others who formed the inner circle of the movement.

Taylor signed with Warner Brothers, keeping Asher as his manager, and released a second album in 1970. As Barney Hoskyns wrote in *Hotel California*, "If one album could be said to have inaugurated the new mellow sound of canyon singer/songwriting, it was Taylor's *Sweet Baby James*."[6] Driven by the popularity of the single "Fire and Rain," Taylor's album achieved record-breaking sales.

In Laurel Canyon, Taylor became integral to a vibrant community of singer/songwriters who worked together, appearing together in concerts and on each other's albums. The Laurel Canyon group was the nucleus of what became a national movement. Not infrequently, musical collaborations led to romance and Taylor was linked to singers Joni Mitchell and then Carly Simon, whom he married in 1972. Simon in turn had previously been linked romantically to musician Cat Stevens and writer/actor/musician Kris Kristofferson.[7]

Taylor was still plagued by substance abuse and, despite his commercial success, interpersonal problems led to the 1983 collapse of his marriage to Simon and the loss of many friends along the way. Taylor eventually overcame his drug problems and married twice more, the last to Caroline Smedvig in 2001.[8] His 1970 breakthrough was the first of many best-selling albums in a career that has lasted into the 21st century.

The singer/songwriter movement illustrates, in some ways, the aftermath of the hippies. Taylor's deeply personal, introspective compositions captured what many analysts saw as a hallmark of the era. Given the bleak economic atmosphere and a "culture of narcissism" fostered by the media, young people turned inward, unsure of what to make of the world around them.[9] This selfish facet of American society in the post-hippie era was largely a response to the youth culture of the sixties.

Taylor's music exemplifies another facet of hippie culture, the desire to get in touch with one's own emotions. Unlike the macho stereotypes of earlier generations, Taylor's appeal was in his sensitivity and his ability to stimulate emotion with his music.

Notes

1. Burt Korall, "James Taylor: Singer-Songwriter," in *The Rock History Reader*, ed. Theo Cateforis (Boca Raton, FL: CRC Press, 2007).

2. Timothy White, *Long Ago and Far Away: James Taylor, His Life and Music* (London: Omnibus Press, 2001).

3. Ian Halperin, *Fire and Rain: The James Taylor Story* (New York: Citadel Press, 2003).

4. White, *Long Ago and Far Away*, 3.

5. Halperin, *Fire and Rain*, 35.

6. Barney Hoskyns, *Hotel California: The True-Life Adventures of Crosby, Stills, Nash, Young, Mitchell, Taylor, Browne, Ronstadt, Geffen, the Eagles, and Their Many Friends* (San Francisco: John Wiley and Sons, 2007), 109.

7. Ibid., 189.

8. Halperin, *Fire and Rain*, xii.

9. Edward D. Berkowitz, *Something Happened: A Political and Cultural Overview of the Seventies* (New York: Columbia University Press, 2006), 158.

The Activists

The activists were the street-level hippie leaders, committed to the political and social values that were the driving force behind the youth movement. Whether involved in political activism or simply working to help hippies on the streets of American cities, the activists were the bridge between the kids on the street and the larger political social movement that shaped 1960s' pop culture.

Robert Peter Cohon "Peter Coyote" (1941–)

Peter Coyote was involved with several prominent San Francisco activist and performance companies in the hippie era, and was one of the founding members of the famous Haight-Ashbury Diggers. Coyote went on to lead a successful career in both film and television, in addition to becoming a successful writer. In 1999 Coyote penned an autobiography of his life and experiences with the Diggers entitled *Sleeping Where I Fall*.

Coyote was born Robert Peter Cohon on October 10, 1941, in New York City, to a middle-class Jewish family. Coyote took an interest in acting in high school and later, while attending Grinnell College in Iowa, became interested in activist politics. Coyote helped to organize a group of 12 students who traveled to Washington D.C. to protest nuclear energy testing and support President John Kennedy's

Hippies attend Steve Gaskin's Monday Night Class to socialize and listen to lectures on spirituality and culture. (© 2009 Robert Altman. Used by permission. Appears in Robert Altman, The Sixties *[Santa Monica Press, 2007].)*

"Peace Race." Coyote and his fellow students were the first protestors to be invited to the White House.[1]

Coyote received his B.A. in English literature from Grinnell, and then moved to the West Coast to attend a graduate program in creative writing at San Francisco State University. After training briefly at the San Francisco Actor's Workshop, Coyote joined the San Francisco Mime Troupe, a traveling theater troupe established in 1959 which performed in public venues around San Francisco.

The Mime Troupe's productions often addressed political and social issues. Because some of the group's acts were seen as obscene, they were denied permits for outdoor performances and, when they performed anyway, they were often arrested. Coyote became one of the troupe's primary writers and directed the troupe's tour and performance of *The Minstrel Show: Civil Rights in a Cracker Barrel*, a blend of jazz, improvisational music, and comedy with a pro–civil rights message.

In 1966 Coyote cowrote *Olive Pits*, an adaptation of Lope de Rueda's *El Paso de las Olivas*, which focused on the problems and pitfalls of material culture and was a major hit for the Mime Troupe, winning the company an Obie Award from New York City's *Village Voice*.[2]

Coyote was one of the founding members of the Diggers, a Haight-Ashbury activist group patterned after a seventeenth-century British society. The Haight-Ashbury incarnation, the brainchild of activist and actor Emmett Grogan, engaged in community activism in an effort to promote a socially conscious type of anarchy. Many of the Diggers' activities were undertaken in anonymity, as it was not their goal to gain fame but rather to change the social order within the makeshift community that had assembled around the Haight.

Despite their controversial and anarchistic aims, the Diggers were one of the most important philanthropic organizations in Haight-Ashbury. They organized sleeping areas for homeless hippies visiting or traveling through the area and created "free stores," where every item was free for the taking to anyone the operators deemed worthy of receiving free goods. The Diggers also distributed free food at the Golden Gate Park panhandle, sometimes serving more than 200 customers using donated (or stolen) food, and threw free parties, organizing entertainment from local rock bands and distributing free drugs to those that attended.[3]

Some of the Diggers, including founder Emmett Grogan, were deeply dissatisfied with the development of the Haight culture in the late 1960s. Grogan believed that, while the hippies originated as a unique cultural movement in search of a new way of life, the culture of the Haight became a free-for-all, overrun with people who did not share the hippie "ideals" and simply came for the drugs, sex, and parties. On October 10, 1967, Coyote's birthday, the Diggers threw a "death of the hippie" march to protest the commercialization of their culture.[4]

Coyote eventually drifted from Grogan and became deeply involved in American Zen Buddhism, dedicating several years of his life to pursuing enlightenment through religious study and practice. While Coyote shifted toward spiritual teachings, the Diggers went on to create the "Free Family," a group that traveled the country and spawned several agrarian communes in the West.[5]

Coyote returned to acting in the late 1970s, appearing in stage productions in California, New York, and elsewhere. His impressive performances eventually landed him roles in feature films, and since 1980 he has worked as an actor full time. In the 21st century, Coyote has also appeared in a number of television programs, including narration and voice work. Reflecting on the significance of the Diggers, Coyote described them with a mix of reverence and stark realism. "Every culture has its priests and devils, its intoxications and follies, and the counterculture we created was neither more nor less ethical, diverse, or contradictory than the majority culture."[6]

Notes

1. Peter Coyote, *Sleeping Where I Fall* (New York: Basic Books, 1999).
2. Susan Vaneta Mason, *The San Francisco Mime Troupe Reader* (Ann Arbor: The University of Michigan Reader, 2005).
3. Coyote, *Sleeping Where I Fall*, 34–40.
4. Ibid., 135.
5. Ibid., 331.
6. Ibid., xiv.

Abbot Howard "Abbie" Hoffman (1936–89)

Abbot "Abbie" Hoffman was a political activist and agitator who headed one of the most prominent activist organizations of the 1960s, the infamous "Yippies." Called the "clown prince of radical protest" in his 1989 obituary in the *New York Times*, Hoffman spent much of the 1960s and 1970s attempting to inspire the spirit of protest among the youth movement, and in the 1980s turned his attention to environmental activism.[1]

Born November 30, 1936, in Worcester, Massachusetts, Hoffman received a graduate degree from the University of California–Berkeley in 1960, where he first took an interest in student activism. In the early 1960s he began working with the Student Nonviolent Coordinating Committee (SNCC), which emerged as one of the most prominent American civil rights organizations in the southern states. Hoffman also organized a small retail store known as "Liberty House," which sold goods produced by cooperatives of poor and homeless craftspeople in the rural South. Hoffman then traveled between New York and California, deeply engaged in the Vietnam protest movement.[2]

In 1968, with fellow activist Jerry Rubin, Hoffman created the Youth International Party, later known as the "Yippies." Hoffman and the Yippies were the first to successfully blend activism into hippie culture, creating a middle ground between the New Left and the everyday hippie who had no clearly defined political connections. Hoffman and the Yippies enticed followers by making political activity fun, combining it with drug use, rock music, and the general party lifestyle of the hip scene.[3]

Hoffman's activism, while based on serious principles, was also comical and lighthearted in comparison to other political movements of the period. Among his various demonstrations, Hoffman and the Yippies promoted a pig (named Pigasus the Immortal) as a presidential candidate in 1968.

In August of 1967, Hoffman and associates entered the gallery of the New York Stock Exchange and dropped money onto the trading floor as a criticism of American capitalism. Hoffman was also one of the masterminds behind the "exorcism of the Pentagon," during which more than 50,000 people gathered in Washington, DC, encircled the Pentagon, and attempted to "levitate" the building using good spiritual vibrations.[4]

Hoffman's radicalism eventually brought him into conflict with the law, when he and Jerry Rubin organized a "Festival of Life" to coincide with and disrupt the 1968 Democratic National Convention in Chicago. The National Mobilization to End the War in Vietnam joined in and more than 2,000 people arrived in Chicago to protest, dance, and hang out in the streets.

Pigasus, the Immortal: Presidential Candidate

The life of Pigasus, the first porcine candidate for president, is shrouded in mystery. Pigasus began life on an Illinois farm before he was purchased (for $20) by the Yippies and became their 1968 presidential nominee. Arrested for being the wrong species to hold office, Pigasus was forcibly prevented from further involvement in politics.

Mayor Richard Daley ordered the police to disperse the crowds, resulting in chaos as protestors and police battled in the streets. Hoffman, Rubin, and five others, who came to be known as the "Chicago Seven," were arrested and charged with conspiracy to incite riots. Though they claimed that their intentions were to create peaceful protest, it was later revealed that Rubin and others had, in fact, supported resisting the police.[5]

Though Hoffman continued his unusual activism well into the 1970s, his popularity peaked with the Chicago Seven trial. Hoffman was arrested in 1973 for possession of cocaine, but fled before his trial, underwent plastic surgery, and went underground, living as "Barry Freed" in Thousand Islands, New York. As Freed, Hoffman became a prominent environmental activist and was even given a commendation by the governor of New York and an appointment to a federal water resources commission.

After seven years in hiding, Hoffman turned himself over to the police and served a year in prison. When he emerged, Hoffman continued working in the environmentalist movement and also traveled the country speaking to students and other activist groups. Hoffman, who had long suffered from serious depression, was active until his 1989 death, from an overdose of barbiturates, which was later ruled a suicide.

While some critics portrayed Hoffman as a publicity hound whose "activism" was motivated by a need for attention, others would argue that it was precisely his ability to inspire and energize people both for and against his activities that made Hoffman effective as an activist and social leader. Biographer Marty Jezer said of Hoffman, "He was one of the best grassroots, seat-of-the-pants community organizers this country has likely ever known; certainly he was its most inventive."[6]

Notes

1. Wayne King, "Abbie Hoffman Committed Suicide Using Barbiturates, Autopsy Shows," *New York Times*, April 19, 1989.
2. Marty Jezer, *Abbie Hoffman: American Rebel* (New Brunswick, NJ: Rutgers University Press, 1992), 20–80.
3. Ibid., 123.
4. King, "Abbie Hoffman," 1.

5. Barry Miles, *Hippie* (New York: Sterling Publishing, 2004), 276.

6. Jezer, *Abbie Hoffman*, xiii.

Hugh Nanton "Wavy Gravy" Romney (1936–)

Hugh Romney, better known by his moniker "Wavy Gravy," was the premier comic activist of the hippie era. Dressed in flamboyant costumes that often included tie-dyed shirts and a variety of unusual hats, Romney appeared at the pop festivals of 1967 and 1968 and at Woodstock in 1969, and was a regular and VIP within the various nooks and crannies of Haight-Ashbury.

Romney was born on May 15, 1936, in Greenbush, New York, and raised in New York City. Romney's first exposure to the counterculture came in Greenwich Village, where he lived and worked, often visiting the coffeehouses and other venues where the new generation of folk singers played. Romney was a friend to Beat celebrities like Bob Dylan and Paul Krassner, and Lenny Bruce served as Romney's manager in the early part of his career.[1]

Before his hippie days, Romney was an art-community radical. Friends described him as well dressed and somewhat conservative in appearance and remarked that he would speak at length about radical and antiestablishment ideals. Romney became a prominent activist on the Lower East Side and was a director of entertainment at the Gaslight Café, a famous venue in New York's folk and alternative music scene.[2]

In 1962 Romney moved to California, where he joined the counterculture of the Haight. He was a sometimes-member of Ken Kesey's Merry Pranksters, and in 1964, he and his second wife founded the Hog Farm Collective, one of the longest-running and most famous counterculture communes.

Originally located on a ranch outside of Los Angeles with a complement of hogs and a few dozen hippies living together, the Hog Farm eventually became a traveling commune, moving from place to place and taking part in a number of prominent events. In his 2007 book *Hippies*, writer Barry Miles quoted Romney as saying of the Hog Farm group, "The Hog Farm is an expanded family, a mobile hallucination, a sociological experiment, and an army of clowns."[3] According to their own records, the Hog farm remained on the road for six years and traveled more than a million miles.

Along the way, Romney began performing as a clown, first as part of his political protest strategy, believing that authorities would be less likely to harm a clown. Romney continued this activity at parties and gatherings throughout the era, often appearing in wild clothes and makeup and telling jokes and stories. The Hog Farm was at the Monterey Pop Festival of 1967 and, the following year, appeared at the demonstrations before the Democratic National Convention in Chicago.

In 1969 organizers of the Woodstock Music and Art Fair asked Romney and the other members of the Hog Farm commune to handle security for the event. Romney and his fellows agreed, saying famously, "My god, they made us the cops." The Hog Farm security had a unique approach to crowd control, using pie fighting and water balloons to ease tensions.[4]

Following Woodstock, Romney and the collective also worked at the Texas Pop Festival of 1970. At the festival Romney shared the stage with B.B. King, who asked if he was called "Wavy Gravy." It was a major moment for Romney, who took an immediate liking to the moniker and eventually decided to change his name legally to Wavy Gravy.

In the early 1970s the Hog Farm Collective traveled through Europe and eventually to Nepal before returning to the United States. Romney remained an activist and a clown throughout the 1970s and 1980s. Along with Richard "Ram Dass" Alpert, Romney was a founding member of the Seva Foundation, and along with his wife he founded Camp Winnarainbow, a circus, improv, and performing arts camp for children. In 1990 Romney ran unsuccessfully for the Berkeley City Council under the slogan "Let's Elect a Real Clown for Change."

In addition to proving one of the most effective activists of the era, Romney's life also provides an example of how the hippie spirit endured in subsequent decades. Romney's comedic activism and his name became symbolic of the lighter side of the generation. Ice cream makers Ben and Jerry later commemorated Romney with a flavor of ice cream named Wavy Gravy in his honor.[5]

Notes

1. William Lawlor, *Beat Culture* (Santa Barbara, CA: ABC-Clio Publishers, 2005).
2. Martin Torgoff, *Can't Find My Way Home: America in the Great Stoned Age* (New York: Simon and Schuster, 2004), 102–6.
3. Barry Miles, *Hippie* (New York: Sterling Publishing, 2004), 270.

4. Ibid., 315.
5. Lawlor, *Beat Culture*, 369.

Jerry Clyde Rubin (1938–94)

Jerry Rubin, who later became famous as a member of the Chicago Seven, was one of the most prominent activist-hippies of the 1960s. Rubin was born on July 14, 1948, in Cincinnati, Ohio, the oldest child of an upper middle-class family. After the death of both parents within 10 months of each other in 1960–61, Rubin was forced to care for his younger brother Gil, then 13.

Rubin entered a graduate program at the University of California–Berkeley in 1964, and though he dropped out of classes some three weeks later, he remained in Berkeley for three years and became deeply involved in student activism. Rubin's success as an activist was largely due to his imaginative approach, including theatrical demonstrations and multimedia aids. When Rubin testified before the House Un-American Activities Committee in 1966, for instance, he wore a Revolutionary War uniform to symbolize his struggle against an oppressive regime.[1]

Early in 1967 Rubin ran for mayor of Berkeley, and though he received only 22 percent of the vote, he gained attention and his participation in the campaign helped to solidify his idea to create a new, radical political party. After his mayoral campaign Rubin began experimenting with LSD and other drugs and spending more time in contact with the grassroots elements of the hippie community. This period of experimentation, and his meeting with fellow activist Abbie Hoffman in 1967, primed Rubin to create the Youth International Party, better known as the "Yippies."[2]

The Yippies staged a number of high-profile stunts, including dropping money on the floor of the New York Stock Exchange, and appeared at dozens of sit-ins and protest rallies. At the 1968 Democratic National Convention in Chicago, Rubin, Hoffman, and their fellows extended an invitation to hippies and activists from around the country to come to Chicago. As usual, the Yippies had a theatrical angle to their protest, and they nominated Pigasus, a pig, as their party's candidate for the presidency.[3]

While many who came to Chicago were more interested in the party than the politics surrounding it, it was one of the largest gatherings of dedicated activists up to that point. Mayor Richard Daley was criticized for ordering police to use violent measures in an effort to control the crowds. On August 23, as Rubin and Hoffman unveiled Pigasus, they and several other prominent Yippie leaders, including the pig, were arrested.

Rubin, Hoffman, and six other defendants were brought to trial on charges of attempting to create a riot and incite violence during the protests in Chicago. Defendant Bobby Seale, a member of the Black Panther Party, was eventually removed from the group and tried separately, leaving the remainder of the group, called the "Chicago Seven," to be tried together.

The trial lasted until February of 1970 and was one of the most widely publicized events of the year. On one day of the trial, Rubin arrived wearing a judicial robe. Though Rubin and his fellow defendants were found innocent of conspiracy, they were convicted of crossing state lines with the intent of causing a riot and sentenced to fines and five years in prison. The sentences were overturned during a retrial in 1972.

Rubin released a book, *Do It: Scenarios of the Revolution*, in 1970, in which he describes many of his ideas about activism and protest in modern American society. The book was successful and he wrote another, *Growing (Up) at Thirty-Seven*, in which he describes portions of his life and his participation in the activism of the 1960s and 1970s.

Rubin was an early investor in Apple Computers and developed, during the late 1970s and 1980s, a view that economic investment was the most practical and effective way to incite social change. In 1994 Rubin was killed by a car while jaywalking on Wilshire Boulevard in Los Angeles. Rubin's writings and his philosophy of economic activism continue to play a role in student activist movements around the country.[4]

Notes

1. David Farber, *Chicago '68* (Chicago: University of Chicago Press, 1994).
2. Ibid., 9.
3. Ibid., 170–71.
4. Catherine L. Albanese, *American Spiritualities: A Reader* (Bloomington: Indiana University Press, 2001), 253–60.

Primary Documents

Studying Hippies

The hippies were, to a large extent, the model for the sociological definition of the term "counterculture." The word came into fashion, within academia, after the publication of historian Theodore Roszak's innovatory 1968 book, *The Making of a Counter Culture*, based on studies of 1960s youth groups in the United States and the United Kingdom. The definition of "counterculture" that emerged from this study was a culture that emerged and existed primarily in opposition to mainstream culture.

This definition places the actions of the hippies within the realm of what sociologists call "deviant behavior," a classification that includes youth groups, criminal cultures, alcoholics, vagrants, hoboes, and any other group whose behavior places them outside the norm. A small group of sociologists, working in the 1960s and 1970s, were the first to subject the hippies to academic scrutiny, and their studies paved the way for the thousands of historical, sociological, and cultural analyses that followed.

1. Interview with Dr. Sherri Cavan

Dr. Sherri Cavan is a professor of sociology at San Francisco State University, an expert in "deviant behavior," and a first-hand witness to the development, growth, and eventual collapse of the San Francisco hippie scene. From her long-time home in the Haight-Ashbury neighborhood of San Francisco, Cavan was well positioned to witness the birth of San Francisco's hippie movement and her training in sociology gave her a tool with which to study the emerging phenomenon.

Cavan conducted one of the first long-term studies of hippie culture, living with the urban hippies in the Haight, and later traveling with hippies as they roamed through California's rural environment looking for communities that would be more accepting of their alternative lifestyle choices. Cavan's 1972 book, Hippies of the Haight, *was a landmark in the study of sixties counterculture and provides one of the first objective views of the Haight-Ashbury community.*

In this interview with the author, conducted on November 19, 2008, at the People's Café in Haight-Ashbury, Dr. Cavan discusses her research, from its origins to her views of counterculture, and the hippies, from a modern perspective.

MI: Dr. Cavan, what were the factors that led you to choose hippies as the subject for your research?

SC: I was living in the neighborhood and so, I kind of like to describe it like a botanist who discovers a new plant species in their back yard. Here I was, a sociologist, and everything was happening around me and so it seemed like a natural progression. My background in sociology was in that amorphous area known as "deviant behavior": rule-breaking and rule-making and rule-enforcing and the consequences of breaching people's expectations and things like that.

MI: What was the Haight-Ashbury neighborhood like before the arrival of the hippies?

SC: In the 1940s, particularly after World War II, there were a lot of union people who made enough money to buy a house or a set of flats and so they began to buy property in this area. By the sixties, the neighborhood had a history of being a working class, open-minded neighborhood. That was one stream that was really important. Also the neighborhood had really cheap rent and the spaces were large. The flats could hold like six or eight people each.

The houses were originally built to accommodate upwardly mobile, upper-class families, kind of like the "McMansions" of their time; the latter part of the end of the nineteenth century. After the Second World War, when there was a large influx in population, a lot of them were broken up into rooming houses.

One of the things that was really important was that the people who were living here were very progressive. More so, even, than the city as a whole. When these strange young people began to appear, the first impulse was like "get them out of here," but at the same time they had a commitment to their own ideology which meant that they couldn't act in that way and they had to be more open. So when they were open, first a few young people came up, then a few more came, then a few more came, and then there was a period of some conflict and the early residents of the neighborhood really began to see that they were losing all control of it. It was no longer a nuclear family neighborhood; it had turned into a young people's ghetto.

At the same time there was kind of an exodus of these original families from the 1940s and 1950s, [who] were moving out to the avenues and out to the suburbs and they were leaving a lot of vacancies. The beats from North Beach had become so congested that they had started to migrate because of cheap rent and large spaces. Those two movements [the Beats and hippies] really just kind of squeezed out of one another.

MI: How did Haight Street change with the arrival of the hippies and the Beats?

SC: One of the big things on Haight Street, there were a bunch of head shops that opened up, and places that had imports from Nepal and all those wonderful things.

There were at least half a dozen independent merchants who set themselves at the opposite to the existing merchant's association. Out of that came the H.I.P. and then Herb Caen, who was a writer for the *San Francisco Chronicle*, coined the term "hippie," and it stuck, though it always had an awkward sound. The "hippies" were just the Haight Independent Merchants.

The Beats didn't think that the hippies were real bohemians, cause they didn't write, they listened to music so, obviously, they weren't real. The merchants were in opposition to the large influx of kids on the street, so there were all these tensions and the "straight" merchants were eventually in opposition to everything.

That's just the way it was, but it was never violent. It didn't get violent around here until the seventies. Certainly, everything began to coalesce into a social movement and there was the whole early media coverage and projected images of what Haight Street and the whole social movement was like, and it began to feed on itself. Eventually it emerged into a fairly vibrant street culture and an enormously successful music scene.

MI: When did you first start to notice the kids arriving?

SC: It was more around 1964 or '65. The way they groomed, the way they dressed and to a certain extent the way they spoke, they really set themselves apart. Never up until that point had there been such a large population, a large demographic population of young people. So, even if the youth movement only appealed to 10 percent of the population, it was a very large 10 percent.

MI: How did you fit into the scene that you were researching?

SC: I was trained as an ethnographer and my doctoral dissertation was on "bar behavior." I wasn't that much older, I was almost 30 then, but I wasn't that much older. The hippies were like from 18 to their twenties, 21, 22, to like 25.

One of the things that happened was there emerged a whole underground economy and there were a number of comic book publishers. Last Gap Press was one of a number of comic book publishers [and was] a big institution in San Francisco. The businesses were like family businesses although the people who participated weren't family in the ordinary sense, they were a collective family. That was a really nice place for me to hang around, to get an inside view of how people operated. I was established as a sort of go-fer because, you see, I had a car, so that made a big difference.

There were things I wouldn't do, like I wouldn't lie and I wouldn't purchase drugs, though I didn't care if people did drugs in front of me. Mainly, I wouldn't lie so they couldn't use me as a cover. They knew that I had a straight life so if they went to court, they thought if someone came who was a professor then that would give more weight. But, I wouldn't do that for them.

One Sunday we all went to the park and they decided, "Oh, let's go smoke some dope." So one of them says, "I know a really good place." So we're climbing along and I looked and I knew that this was not a really good place, because the logs we had to climb over were already really smooth and it was evident that a lot of people had already climbed over those. So I thought, "Okay." Through the bushes come these motorcycle cops, and everybody stops. So then they started looking at IDs and looking at mine, I'm 32 years old, and the cop says, "Lady, get outta here."

MI: Was there a significant drug culture in Haight-Ashbury before the hippies arrived?

SC: No, there was a big bar culture. Part of the early population was an Irish population and so there were all sorts of pubs. The Beats may have brought some of the drugs with them, but it was very different. What smoking marijuana did to the Beats was very different from what smoking marijuana did to the hippies. The entire belief system and culture molds the experience that you have.

MI: What happened to change the scene?

SC: I think that the big thing that happened was the types of drugs that came into the neighborhood changed—heroin and speed—because before that it was mushrooms, marijuana, and mescaline. Hard drugs started to come in and when they came in there was a lot of violence. I didn't know then as much as I know now, but now I understand that hard drugs moved into a lot of areas of the country around that time. For example, the introduction of cocaine into the black community was happening about the same time.

I have nothing against conspiracy theories, I mean, some of them must be right. It was believed at that time, and a little later, that this was a purposeful plot and that it was the idea to totally demoralize these communities and then they would be done with them and wouldn't have to deal with them. The story of how hard drugs came to America is interesting in its own right and played a role.

The amount of violence increased and the city of San Francisco really started to get nasty. There was violence on the street and there were "bad vibes." A different category of people started to emerge. Businesses started to close down and, you know you see the metal grates [security grates on the entrances of buildings], these began to appear at this time. Where I lived, on the corner there was a corner grocery store and two blocks down there was another grocery store, and within the period of a month, the grocers in both of those stores had been killed in robberies. I felt like someone in a western movie, like watching them shootin' it out in the street.

MI: What happened to the hippies that were living here?

SC: What happened was that some people just said, oh you know, this ideology is not worth anything and you can't sustain it in this world and you might as well just go back to the straight world, and they did. Others, who were committed to the belief system itself, began to spread out into the country.

There were communes and then there were free-ranging hippies and then there were "villagers" and the villagers were very analogous to the ones that moved into the Haight in the early days because these places were listed in the country records as ghost towns, they had lost so much of their population, and the only people that were left were these old people, in their sixties, seventies, and eighties. Suddenly, coming down the road were all these young people. So the old people, they didn't like the way they [the hippies] dressed and they didn't like the way they talked and they didn't like the way they smoked, but, if you needed someone to help you fix the roof . . .

So they developed this very interesting symbiotic relationship in the villages themselves and then there were communes in the mountains and there was a connection between the "communards" and the "villagers" and then there were wandering hippies that were constantly on the road. In the village that I was at, the old guys made a distinction between "our hippies" and the "dirty hippies." The ones in the village that helped with the work and who they knew on a one-to-one basis were the good hippies.

These were people who were committed to the ideology and committed to the belief system, but came to believe that you just couldn't do it in the city. There were just too many forces acting against you in the city and so that was really the beginning of the whole "back to the land" movement and early ecology movement. There was an idea that you could just "liberate space," to move in and make it yours. All up and down the coast, from Eureka to San Diego. In an opportunistic way, like, whenever there was an opportunity, it was the same as in the Haight, when there was vacant housing and cheap rents.

In the Haight they were also opportunistic, like in those days you could "job share." Not formally, but a lot of people worked in the postal office, that was a favorite one because it was civil service and it paid regularly and you were on your own and worked outside. So, often, in a household there would be two or three strains of income. Someone had a job and somebody was getting money from home and there would be somebody on welfare and there would be somebody who was selling dope and they would share income.

In the context of the larger society, it's a difficult life and belief system to sustain. It's much easier to collapse into the arms of the conventional culture. Part of the breakdown is that people discovered that living on the edge with very little money is really hard and they would look around and see people with straight jobs and so I think there was a certain sense that it was breaking down, because of a lot of factors.

MI: What happened to the original residents after the hippie buildup?

SC: Some of them left and some are still here. Some are still active in the neighborhood council. Many people, including myself, have a very strong attachment to the area and that, of course, was something that the hippies used to say, that this was a very "powerful spot," but it is. When the drugs came and a lot of the hippies left, a lot of the straights left, too, because it was really ugly. You didn't go out after dark.

It's become a *place* and there's an enormous influx of tourists from all over the world, [coming] just to walk down the street and take their picture with the sign that says Haight-Ashbury. It's like Waterloo, or like those historic places.

MI: What is the difference between what "hippie" meant back then and what it means now?

SC: I think young people are always the bearers of the counterculture. I don't think that the counterculture springs from middle-aged or older people. Constantly new generations of young people responding in different ways, like the emergence of punk, which was about the time of the end of the vibrant hippie era.

In the fifties and early sixties, before the hippies had emerged, and the Beatles were right on the edge, there was a whole movement of the "mods" and "rockers." And, in the mods, fashion was based on like 18th-century dandies. Occasionally, something will emerge de Nuevo, having no relation to anything else, but there is a tendency to recycle. But, usually not the next generation because you hate your parents; you rebel.

MI: What are the lasting remnants of the hippie culture in our society?

SC: Lots of things from recreational drugs, styles of music, free love, and breaking down the sexual mores of the fifties. The whole green movement and the notion of living lightly. That was one of the consequences of it. It was very powerful and maybe because they were onto something. The idea of love not war, for instance, is still a counterculture in our society. Beyond the superficial examples of hairstyles and the introduction of "tie dye" as a color, I think there were really genuine insights.

I sort of subscribe to a pendulum view of history, like things they move and they get so far out, and then they sort of come back and that is what we're hopefully experiencing now.

I think that I was substantively changed by doing that research. Even though I had done all this research on bars which, you know, roughed me up a little, I was inspired farther and farther left and, in all these years, I've never found a reason to leave that position. When you're really trying to understand something, you either say "I understand it and it's a crock of s***," or "I really understand it and it's a worthwhile way to proceed."

2. Conclusion from "Class Structure of Hippie Society"

The following is an excerpt from Dr. Cavan's article "The Class Structure of Hippie Society," published in the October 1972 issue of Urban Life and Culture. *In the article, Cavan explains the hippies as a culture in the process "counter-development," wherein the hippies attempted to simplify the structure of their society whereas most cultures develop by way of increasing complexity. Cavan's analysis focuses on the underground economy and divides hippie groups into various classes of workers and earners, including "craftsmen," "peddlers," and "merchants," each with differing levels of status within hip society.*

This excerpt is provided primarily as an example of the tone and format of academic work on hippies. In addition, Cavan's analysis is

interesting because her focus on economy, as one measure of community inte-
gration, is a prime example of the way in which sociologists attempt to
quantify complex social and cultural groups. Cavan's analysis, though not
provided in its entirety, is therefore a valuable exploration of how the
hippie phenomenon was fueled by practical concerns, like the collection and
distribution of resources.

Hippie society is ideally conceived of as a place where personal interest is served; where the individual is free to "do his own thing" and
to "find where he's at." In its utopian version, it is a world where each,
in accordance with personal disposition, acts in terms of his individual
interests; and all, in sharing similar interests, act in concert. Thus
how any individual chooses to orient himself toward the means of
production and distribution ultimately rests on matters of personal
disposition. Some hippies live as idlers, as persons who drift aimlessly,
without ambition. Others homestead and focus their attention on
"getting by." Yet others desire to secure various advantages for themselves and their kin—and in so desiring they may direct their attention and interest towards the marketplace.

Resources—whether they be skill or cash, stamina or guile—are
what the individual brings to the marketplace. Regardless of how he
came by them, resources provide bargaining power. Where resources
are scant, the individual's position in the market situation is low, and
what assets he has are likely to be expropriated by others. Those
whose resources are more substantial are correspondingly more free to
pursue life in accordance with personal disposition. And they sometimes do so at a profit.

Resources are also necessary to build a new society. The hippies
constitute a subordinate culture that must engage in daily transactions
with the dominant group. The alternatives they have available for the
reconstruction of societal forms are those that are compatible with, if
not identical to, the dominant culture. So, even though they make
frequent use of barter among themselves, their transactions with the
conventional culture necessitate a source of revenue. The three main
sources of revenue in hippie society are public assistance, family allot-
ments and members' own labor. Within the context of members' own
labor would include dealing dope, rip-offs, and business.

In the present paper, I have focused only on business. Business
holds an important place in the new society. It is used to supplement

revenue from other sources, even where it does not supplant them. It accounts for the largest cash flow in the counter-culture. Finally, though economic exchange, business brings together large numbers of individuals in routinized patterns of conduct. In turn, these routine patterns of economic exchange create a particular societal form: the underground marketplace.

As Belshaw (1965) [*Traditional Exchange and Modern Markets*] notes with respect to peasant economies, the market does not come into existence to enable persons to dispose of surplus. It comes into existence as a function of the division of labor. The mode this division takes among the hippies is five class-like social groups: vagabonds (explained in the article as individuals who drift between settlements in a nomadic fashion), peddlers, craftsmen, merchants, and entrepreneurs.

Craftsmanship forms the backbone of the underground economy and the skilled craftsman holds the most esteemed place in hippie society. Ideally, his creativity is an expressive rather than instrumental act. But nonetheless, it is understood that he has the right to market his wares. It is also understood that some craftsmen do not desire to market their own wares directly, and hence arrangements for distribution exist. Both peddlers and merchants act as traders within the economy, although these two groups are distinguished from one another in a variety of ways: by the complexity and permanence of their enterprise, by the dominant nature of their repute in both the counter-culture and the dominant culture, and by their relations with the class of craftsmen.

This complex of three roles forms the core of the economy. Between them, goods are produced and distributed and money begins to circulate. However, the underground market extends beyond this core, to incorporate vagabonds, whose personal assets consist of interest, if not skill, and entrepreneurs, whose personal interest goes beyond trade to promotion.

Movement across these class lines is fluid. Craftsmen may peddle their own wares; vagabonds may learn a skill; merchants and entrepreneurs are sometimes interchangeable. However, the classes exist as observable features of the underground marketplace. They constitute concrete forms of exchange that have become routinized in the counter-culture, and, in their routinization, they have provided that culture with some measure of economic stability.

Yet that measure of economic stability comes at a cost to cultural consistency. In the context of "ordinary business," values stressed by the ideology are subverted by everyday practice. Principles of altruism begin to give way to those of chicanery; bluffing replaces up-front transactions; planning and organization supplant spontaneity and psychic whim.

Source: Excerpt from Sherri Cavan, "The Class Structure of Hippie Society," *Urban Life and Culture* (October 1972): 235–37. © 1972 Sage Publications. Used by permission of Sherri Cavan and Sage Publications.

Hip Media: Spreading the Word

The "hip media" was the subset of print and broadcast media produced for, and in many cases by, members of hip society. The press included dozens of magazines, newspapers, comic books, and radio programs, which mirrored the mainstream press, often covering the same stories, but angling their content toward the tastes and preferences of the new consumer market. Every facet of the hip media industry, from the hiring processes of managers and editors to the advertisers chosen to sell their goods in hip papers and on hip radio, was strategically organized to cater to the ideals of hip culture.

Often self-celebratory, the press presented hip culture as an elixir for the disease that was deteriorating the integrity and harmony of mainstream America. The products of the hip press were often poorly produced and lacking in quality, but were more about form than function. The hip media was rarely satisfied to produce news; it sought to create "art."

While the counterculture press flourished around the country, the following articles are taken from San Francisco's *The Oracle*, which is widely recognized as one of the premier hippie publications.

3. "The Gathering of the Tribes"

One of the primary functions of the counterculture press was to let hippies on the street know what was "happening" in the scene. The hip papers were the primary promotional tool for the organizers of hippie society and any event, from readings by hip authors at coffeehouses to political protests, were spread through the counterculture press.

This article, published in the January 1967 issue of The Oracle, *advertises the Human Be-In, one of the first grand gatherings of hippie icons in San Francisco. While this short article is presented without its original formatting and illustrative accompaniment, the language used by the writer provides an example of how advertisers and promoters attempted to appeal to the attitudes of hip society. In its original format, this short article appeared under an image created by graphic designer Stanley "Mouse" Miller, known for blending pseudo Native American tribal motifs with photos of hippies, and promoter Chet Helms, who was largely responsible for organizing the event.*

A union of love and activism previously separated by categorical dogma and label mongering will finally occur ecstatically when Berkeley political activists and hip community and San Francisco's spiritual generation and contingents from the emerging revolutionary generation all over California meet for a Gathering of the Tribes for a Human Be-In at the Polo Field in Golden Gate Park on Saturday, January 14, 1967, from 1 to 5 P.M.

Twenty to fifty thousand people are expected to gather for a joyful Pow-Wow and Peace Dance to be celebrated with leaders, guides, and heroes of our generation: Timothy Leary will make his first Bay Area public appearance; Allen Ginsberg will chant and read with Gary Snyder, Michael McClure, and Lenore Kandel; Dick Alpert, Jerry Rubin, Dick Gregory, and Jack Weinberg will speak. Music will be played by all the Bay Area rock bands, including the Grateful Dead, Big Brother and the Holding Co., Quicksilver Messenger Service, and many others. Everyone is invited to bring costumes, blankets, bells, flags, symbols, cymbals, drums, beads, feathers, flowers.

Now in the evolving generation of America's young the humanization of the American man and woman can begin in joy and embrace without fear, dogma, suspicion, or dialectical righteousness. A new concert of human relations being developed within the youthful underground must emerge, become conscious, and be shared so that a revolution of form can be filled with a Renaissance of compassion, awareness, and love in the Revelation of the unity of all mankind. The Human Be-In is the joyful, face-to-face beginning of the new epoch.

Source: "The Gathering of the Tribes," *The Oracle*, no. 5 (January 1967): 90. © 2005 Regent Press. Used by permission of Mark Weiman, as originally printed in *The Oracle*, and collected in the book/CD/DVD *The San Francisco Oracle: The Psychedelic Newspaper of the Haight Ashbury.*

Hip Media: Protecting the Community

The hip press also filled an important function by forming a bridge between hip culture and the outside world. Developments in the national media were reproduced in the hip press, after being given the appropriate alternations in language and style. The papers also tried to help hippies avoid conflict with, among other groups, the police. Many hip papers published photos of undercover police and reported on arrests to help hippies avoid placing themselves in situations that would lead to legal conflict.

In the following articles, both published in 1966 in the pages of The Oracle, *we see examples of the hip press engaged in one of the primary functions of all media: transmitting news and information to the population. In the first, editor Allen Cohen relays a story about a meeting between police and the Haight–Ashbury community, showing how, in some cases, mainstream authority and the hip community could reach out to one another, using dialogue to avoid conflict. In the second article, an unidentified writer shares a story about an attempted police crackdown in the Haight and the reaction on the street, which included the oft-favored strategy of the "counter protest."*

4. "Haight-Ashbury Meets Police"

Two plainclothes officers of the Police Community Relations Unit appeared at the I/and Thou Coffee House on Wednesday, September 14, at the invitation of David Rothkop, the owner, in one of a series of bi-weekly community dialogues.

Officers Jones and Blackstone jovially, openly, and intelligently countered a barrage of questions from a crowd of 120 people, ranging from the bearded and bare-footed to grey-haired ladies, professors, lawyers, and other concerned citizens of the Haight-Ashbury.

The questions articulated a passionate concern over police harassment and brutality by members of the Park District police station. The officers admitted police harassment and brutality and that "the wheels of justice are not always just" (Jones): and that the

Community Relations detail could only affirm and clarify the impartiality of the law but couldn't justify or defend individual acts, biases, or attitudes of 1,800 policemen.

Officer Blackstone stated the main police problem in the Haight-Ashbury was possession of marijuana and then holding up a cigarette said, "I've probably got a more deadly narcotic in my hand than pot, but that's not what the law says." The two officers parried all questions, harangues and pleas from the heated, tightly packed audience with a coolness to be envied by all hipsters. Everyone agreed that they were the best "good guys" the police could find. Jones admitted the subjectivity and prejudices of policemen on the beat. "Some policemen will look at your face, decide you're a crook and arrest you," he said.

Speaking of a citizen's rights while in public he said, "If not arrested you can refuse to be searched and go on your way but I can't promise you what will happen after that." He stated that all who feel they have been harassed by the police should file a complaint at the Hall of Justice. All complaints are investigated and listed in each officer's records.

Members of Citizens Alert who have been collecting information and filing complaints on police harassment and brutality, indicated that in 18 months of activity, they have received only 8 official replies, all dismissing their complaints as unfounded.

The meeting continually stumbled into the same impasse of police prejudice and hostility against the new bohemians in the Haight-Ashbury, which has caused illegal, unjust, and often brutal search and seizure. Jones suggested that it is "the responsibility of the community to keep the police as clean as possible." This lead to suggestions that Haight-Ashbury citizens have an opportunity to confront Captain Kiely and members of the Park District Police Station in an open meeting, to discuss community problems. Jones said that such a meeting could probably be arranged if a written request were sent to Chief Cahill and a cover letter to the Community Relations Unit. It was resolved by all those present that the request would be drafted and sent. Members of the audience then advised the officers that if dialogue between police and community did not improve, the community would resort to more drastic measures against illegal and brutal law enforcement, including open petitions, picketing of the police station and police surveillance teams.

Finally the officers were asked why pictures were taken of all the peace marchers and demonstrations; under what mandate and in investigation of what crime. Blackstone replied that the Intelligence Division, whose job it is to gather information, took and filed the pictures, but that he has no idea what the pictures were used for and that anyone interested could ask the Intelligence Division.

Source: Allen Cohen, "Haight Ashbury Meets Police," *The Oracle*, no. 1 (September 20, 1966): 17. © 2005 Regent Press. Used by permission of Mark Weiman, as originally printed in *The Oracle*, and collected in the book/CD/DVD *The San Francisco Oracle: The Psychedelic Newspaper of the Haight Ashbury*.

5. "The Action"

About 5 in the afternoon a slowly cruising squad car did an angry u-turn &, with 5 gunbarrels poked out its windows, stopped it's swerve abruptly in front of a young long haired, bearded man with yellow boots & a blonde, long haired girl. "Get off this street, boy— NOW," "git," another voice from within, and a mumbled—"damn niggers," for the boy was brown skinned and he & his fair maid were on Haight & Ashbury on this sunny afternoon—a street filled with laughing people except when truckloads of bayonet wielding troops & beef & bullet stuffed police cars stalked the street.

Actually the people were not afraid of black teenagers—our neighbors—but raw power seeking opposition to crush—King John [sons'] deputies . . .

About 7:30, the "merry men" (about 30 in strength), wielding picket signs:—Cops go home, support love, & no more curfew— walked up & down Haight street. The fear & tension subsided, people looked & laughed—others joined in, and the normal night time Haight Street sounds were heard again.

By 8:00 P.M. the crowd had swelled to about 200 children, hippies & just bystanders. At 8:05 a fire engine w/siren blasting roared up Haight Street. When it got to Cole the crowd stopped and turned to look. What they saw was a wall of club wielding blue uniforms followed by olive drab riflemen with poised bayonets coming down Haight St. The surprised people were herded down the street, some into waiting paddy wagons & city buses. The cops weren't brutal but they were frighteningly cold.

I walked toward them & thru them—was almost busted—but my guardian angel (temporarily acquired) looked straight enough to get us through. Looking back we could see the roadblock they'd set up at Masonic and herded people towards a nice efficient trap.

Then as an empty bus came past the police loudspeaker system began to work—it was all over. In trying to call for information on those busted the only answer was—"no information" & "get off the phone." So ended the "great" Haight-Ashbury police action.

Source: "The Action," *The Oracle* 1, no. 2, p. 3. © 2005 Regent Press. Used by permission of Mark Weiman, as originally printed in *The Oracle*, and collected in the book/CD/DVD *The San Francisco Oracle: The Psychedelic Newspaper of the Haight Ashbury.*

Hip Media: Philosophy in Print

In addition to its function as a source of information, the hip press was also charged with disseminating the philosophy of hip culture. Toward this end, counterculture papers often invited articles about various philosophical, spiritual, and cultural schools that appealed to the hippie worldview. It was common for hip papers to run articles on Eastern spirituality, Native American traditions, and other popular "new schools," and it was also common for the papers to instruct their readers on how to live the hip life and avoid the perils of banal, mainstream existence.

In the article below, from the February 1967 issue of the San Francisco Oracle, *author Tom Law provides a "mantra" for hippie life, culminating in his belief that hippies would eventually leave urban environments to form agricultural communities, with their former urban enclaves serving as "ports" where hippies would remain in contact with the straight world. In addition to providing an example of how hippie philosophy was presented in the counterculture press, Law articulates a rapidly spreading sentiment among the hippies: urban life and hippie life were largely incompatible. These ideas were mirrored in the philosophy of the Back to the Land movement and by those who went on to form the rural hippie communes and villages of the 1970s.*

6. "The Community of the Tribe"

In this phase of our organic growth we must all center, letting the forces and energies that are happening within us draw us together. By doing so we render impotent the cop without as well as the cop within.

We must then consciously enforce that centering to avoid the ugly games of power and prejudice which erode the community spirit, feeling, and effort. In times of decision this centering is the process of dipping, beyond images of the intellect, into the wellspring of the divine within every man and there finding the next natural step in the process of creating our new world. We thereby respect each other and the environment which we find ourselves creating for the Tribe. The Tribe then is. Without pushing or pointing it grows organically.

The organic growth of love and cooperation in us is the balancing factor of nature. To every facet of hate we must reflect love and to know this we must practice it unceasingly in all directions.

Guard carefully against feeling that we are a special, new or unique tribe. We are the ancient tribal consciousness of man in harmonious relationship with nature. The distended machine is the mutant.

We are all—squares and the psychedelically enlightened alike—involved in our world of now. To take up the call, to respond to the cosmic forces, we must *be* the hard-working, harmonious, respectful, honest, diligent, co-operative family of man. Our words are inspired. Our devotion is strong. The precious revelations which have come through us with increasing magnitude must be fathomed until we are one with each other and can extend our awareness beyond the tribe to our entire planet.

What is the natural karmic duty of a generation whose brother, neighbors, and childhood friends now promote hate by killing innocent human beings around the world? It is to balance their jive and immature actions with the light of intelligent goodness; fearlessly to deal with the money-mad machine in order to release its hold on our bowels—the bowels of mankind.

Practically, this means that all excess profit is turned back into the community. That means all money, material things, food, etc., which are beyond the basic necessities of a happy, healthy, human existence: loyal to the turn-on. While profit is only to be made on those people led and fed by the machine.

By more and more of us approaching this new level of awareness within, and by giving to each other, we quite naturally are open to receive. We all become our creative selves, creating our society within this massive mess of victims of greed, indulgence, possessiveness, and hate. If our souls are mirrors, does not hate reflect hate?

So we must change the entire environment, dealing within and for the community which we create. *Do* that love with those who'll do love with you: the promoter, artist, editor, concessionaire, musician, shopkeeper, carpenter, plumber, dishwasher cook, monk, and all the other masters of smoke, color, and the all-knowing center. Without offending the Plastic-Zip population, we can create our own communities and ashrams and love environments where we can turn on and tune into the real cosmic dream of awakening, once again, to nature; where we can live in health within our needs both practical and spiritual.

Let's make Haight Love together, and then move to the country where love is hanging out waiting. Love-Ashbury will then exist as our trade capital, our funnel to the world, and we can occasionally share a natural sunset together, steadying our lives with both the active and the passive changes.

Source: Tom Law, "The Community of the Tribe," *The Oracle*, no. 6 (February 1967): 15. © 2005 Regent Press. Used by permission of Mark Weiman, as originally printed in *The Oracle*, and collected in the book/CD/DVD *The San Francisco Oracle: The Psychedelic Newspaper of the Haight Ashbury.*

7. Interview with Robert Altman

Photographers, both in the hip press and in the mainstream media, were an essential component in the spread of hip culture. A young woman living in St. Louis, Missouri, for instance, might decide to wear a feathered boa after seeing a photo of Janis Joplin doing likewise in a magazine spread. A group of students might similarly be moved to protest after seeing pictures of thousands of hippies gathered in Central Park for an anti-Vietnam march. While hip literature spread sentiments and ideals, photos spread the hippie aesthetic, from clothing and hairstyles to posture and attitude.

Over more than 40 years as a photographer, Robert Altman has recorded the ebb and flow of pop culture, from the enigmatic street scenes of Greenwich Village to rock 'n' roll culture of the sixties, seventies, and eighties. Altman, whose photos appear throughout this book, was the second chief photographer for Rolling Stone *magazine and catalogued images of some of the hippie era's brightest stars, including Janis Joplin, Grace Slick, Jim Morrison, David Crosby, Abbie Hoffman, and Jerry Garcia. He is the author of the book* The Sixties, *which contains many of his now-iconic images of that era's culture and music scene.*

In this interview, conducted on December 2, 2008, Altman speaks about becoming a photographer, the hippie scene in New York and San Francisco, and the relevance of sixties counterculture in the modern era.

MI: How did you start photographing hippies?

RA: I was a psychology major in college and grew up as a practical person, believing in science and weight and measure and I was not cosmic or ethereal at all. And I was looking for something creative to do, instead of becoming a psychologist or an attorney or a scientist.

I tried playing guitar and becoming a rock star but I did not have the talent for that, clearly, so I found photography itself. I was living in New York City, in the East Village, and we had a psychedelic shop that we opened up and there was space on the wall and I got into photography as part of my quest for something creative. I took photographs of my friends, 'cause I thought they were colorful, and I put them on the wall of this psychedelic shop and a number of people came up and said, "These are really great photographs." So that slap on the back gave me what I needed, confidence and assurance that I was okay at this. So I proceeded to take more photographs.

MI: How were you a participant in the counterculture?

RA: I never considered myself a hippie, because "hippie" is a word which kind of denigrates what you could be, in my opinion. My friends in college used to say, "I'm not a hippie but I am hip."

I certainly was a member of the counterculture and a culture which was trying to redefine how to live a life and not just accept the white bread, boring plan that our 1950s parents had set out for us and that their parents had set out for them. We all, as a huge group of people, kind of figured [it] out together and communicated to each other through alternative press, music (Dylan and the Beatles, etc.), films, underground radio, and just meeting at be-ins and small parties and in small circles of friends. We were very aware of each other and that there were a lot of us and that we actually had power and influence. And it was fun. It was a lot of fun.

MI: How did you start working for *Rolling Stone*?

RA: *Rolling Stone* was a very young magazine at the time. It must have been two years old. I originally started working at a paper called the *San Francisco Express Times*, which then became the *San Francisco Good Times*. It was one of about three or four papers in the Bay Area, one of about 180 alternative press newspapers around the country. It was considered, stylistically, one of the absolute best. The only one that was probably a little bit better was *The Oracle*.

Rolling Stone did a story about the counterculture press. It was written by a fella named John Birch, who was the managing editor of *Rolling Stone*, and he cited me as one of the three best photographers in the country. He called me a "Pollyanna." Then I did an interview with Peter Fonda and Dennis Hopper, who had just done *Easy Rider*, and *Rolling Stone* bought a photograph from me, of Peter Fonda, so that started the relationship. Then at some point, the first photographer, Baron Wolman, he was easing out the door and there was a niche to be filled and I was invited to become their staff photographer.

MI: Who are some of the memorable hippie celebrities you photographed?

RA: My first subject was Jim Morrison of the Doors. That was fascinating. He had these leather trousers, and I never saw leather pants before. And I never saw long hair on a man before. In those days you had access; you could walk right up and take pictures. These days you'd be clubbed by security.

Janis Joplin, I was working for *Rolling Stone* at that point, and they wanted me to shoot with her. So I called her up at three in the afternoon, *three in the afternoon*, right, and she, froggy voice, gets on the phone, "Man, do you know what time it is?" Click.

As a photographer, I'm very sensitive and one of my natural abilities is that I like people and I revere certain people. So, I'm putting out a very positive vibe and people get that I'm okay and that they're okay and that it's okay to be photographed. That enables some special things that occur in front of my camera. I'm also good at capturing the "decisive moment," when all the elements come together.

MI: What happened to the hippies, in your opinion?

RA: Well, all children grow up, even flower children. Ideas change and experiences change you. Some people say that the "Death of [the] Hippie" happened in a demonstration sometime in 1967. I came here in '68 and I didn't see any death, I saw a lot of life, so for me the sixties didn't end until the mid-seventies. John Lennon said that the sixties ended at Altamont, December 6, 1969. He used the expression, "The bubble burst."

MI: What was the significance of the hippies?

RA: Well, it was very well put by Abbie Hoffman. To poorly paraphrase it, "We didn't win the war but we won a lot of battles," which included the fact that you just can't draft half a million kids and send them off to an unpopular war. We ended that. Even though, kids are going off to Iraq, they're doing that voluntarily. There's a huge difference between someone yanking you out of your life and putting you in harm's way and asking you to kill people who you have nothing against.

We brought attention to the fact that the environment was in serious trouble. It was our generation, the counterculture, and no one else's. Before Al Gore, who didn't invent the green world or green consciousness. We brought out the idea that women are not second-class citizens and our thinking helped spurn the feminist movement.

We were arrogant, we were reckless, we were silly, we were scared to death, and we were right.

I think that the hippie period will always be looked on as a historic point in time. I think that the influences will always be here, I hope and I pray. It looked for a while that Bush turned us away from all the advances we made and look where we are today, we have hope. Hope has returned. It's like the day before Kennedy got shot, which to me is the day when the world changed. If Kennedy didn't get shot we wouldn't have had the same hippie movement but my world changed the moment that Kennedy was shot.

MI: The most memorable event you attended?

RA: The most cherished, fun, memorable event for me was the 1968 Easter Be-In in Central Park at Sheep's Head Meadow. I and my friends helped organize that and we got there at dawn. You'd hear a flute a thousand yards away and a tambourine. There would be like, 10 people, and then 15 and then 500 and then 5,000. They were tripping on LSD and they were laughing and smiling. We were young, and we had endless future in front of us. We were pretty, at least we thought we were.

There is a place in Sheep's Head Meadow, a rock where you could sit on, and that was kind of "ground zero." For a lot of that day I was sitting there, on that rock, with the entire Be-In spread before me. My friend Allison, who had this big hat on and was holding daffodils, she kept saying, "it doesn't matter, it just doesn't matter." And it really didn't.

I once had the temerity to rewrite the Ten Commandments and I called it the "Ten Suggestions." The last one, number 10, was "Have a good time." I think that we do our job and be responsible and keep our agreements with people, then, let's have a good time, too.

Politics of Hippieism

The political environment of 1960s America was the source of much of the hippies' angst and disillusionment. From the Vietnam conflict to the Black Panthers and the feminists, legitimate political movements around the world fed into hippie culture. While the political issues facing the country were serious, the hippies often made light of the subject, preferring to parody the establishment, rather than engage in substantive action or protest.

Serious sixties revolutionaries might have laughed at the very idea of "hippie activism," as the hippies were not known for doing much other than hanging out and "doing their own thing." In most cases, "their own thing" did not involve activism. In a few cases, however, groups sprung up that blurred the lines between activist and hippie. One example is the Diggers, a grassroots activist organization that grew out of the street scene in San Francisco. Patterned after a 17th-century English communist organization, the SF Diggers were interested in encouraging the new, emerging culture to make a complete break with their parent culture and create an urban utopia in which the rules of property, ownership, and commerce were no longer relevant.

Within the Haight-Ashbury community, the Diggers functioned as a philanthropic organ, distributing free food and goods to the hippies on the street, goods that they sometimes "liberated" from merchants who did not share the Diggers' new view of ownership. This Digger philosophy of free goods for free people culminated in the Free Store, an organization where Diggers volunteers distributed goods and food, free of charge, to anyone who wanted them.

The following article, "Trip Without a Ticket," is considered a "Digger Manifesto" and was originally published in the winter of 1966–67. The article later became part of "The Digger Papers," in 1968, and was included by archivist Eric Noble in his web-based collection of Diggers documents at www.diggers.org. Written in a meandering, stream-of-consciousness style, the document explains the Diggers' ideas behind the establishment of the Free Store, the argument against ownership and property, and the Digger lifestyle as "street theater."

8. "Trip Without a Ticket"

Our authorized sanities are so many Nembutals. "Normal" citizens with store-dummy smiles stand apart from each other like cotton-packed capsules in a bottle. Perpetual mental out-patients. Maddeningly sterile jobs for strait-jackets, love scrubbed into an insipid "functional personal relationship" and Art as a fantasy pacifier. Everyone is kept inside while the outside is shown through windows: advertising and manicured news. And we all know this.

How many TV specials would it take to establish one Guatemalan revolution? How many weeks would an ad agency require to face-lift the image of the Viet Cong? Slowly, very slowly we are led nowhere. Consumer circuses are held in the ward daily. Critics are tolerated like exploding novelties. We will be told which burning Asians to take seriously. Slowly. Later.

But there is a real danger in suddenly waking a somnambulistic patient. And we all know this.

What if he is startled right out the window?

No one can control the single circuit-breaking moment that charges games with critical reality. If the glass is cut, if the cushioned distance of media is removed, the patients may never respond as normals again. They will become life-actors.

Theater is territory. A space for existing outside padded walls. Setting down a stage declares a universal pardon for imagination. But what happens next must mean more than sanctuary or preserve. How would real wardens react to life-actors on liberated ground? How can the intrinsic freedom of theater illuminate walls and show the weakspots where a breakout could occur?

Guerrilla theater intends to bring audiences to liberated territory to create life-actors. It remains light and exploitative of forms for the same reasons that it intends to remain free. It seeks audiences that are created by issues. It creates a cast of freed beings. It will become an issue itself.

This is theater of an underground that wants out. Its aim is to liberate ground held by consumer wardens and establish territory without walls. Its plays are glass cutters for empire windows.

Free store/property of the possessed.

The Diggers are hip to property. Everything is free, do your own thing. Human beings are the means of exchange. Food, machines, clothing, materials, shelter and props are simply there. Stuff. A perfect dispenser would be an open Automat on the street. Locks are time-consuming. Combinations are locks.

So a store of goods or clinic or restaurant that is free becomes a social art form. Ticketless theater. Out of money and control.

"First you gotta pin down what's wrong with the West. Distrust of human nature, which means distrust of Nature. Distrust of wildness in oneself literally means distrust of Wilderness."—Gary Snyder.

Diggers assume free stores to liberate human nature. First free the space, goods and services. Let theories of economics follow social facts. Once a free store is assumed, human wanting and giving, needing and taking, become wide open to improvisation.

A sign: If Someone Asks to See the Manager Tell Him He's the Manager.

Someone asked how much a book cost. How much did he think it was worth? 75 cents. The money was taken and held out for anyone. "Who wants 75 cents?" A girl who had just walked in came over and took it.

A basket labeled Free Money.

No owner, no Manager, no employees and no cash-register. A salesman in a free store is a life-actor. Anyone who will assume an answer to a question or accept a problem as a turn-on.

Question (whispered): "Who pays the rent?"

Answer (loudly): "May I help you?"

Who's ready for the implications of a free store? Welfare mothers pile bags full of clothes for a few days and come back to hang up dresses. Kids case the joint wondering how to boost.

Fire helmets, riding pants, shower curtains, surgical gowns and World War I Army boots are parts for costumes. Nightsticks, sample cases, water pipes, toy guns and weather balloons are taken for props. When materials are free, imagination becomes currency for spirit.

Where does the stuff come from? People, persons, beings. Isn't it obvious that objects are only transitory subjects of human value? An object released from one person's value may be destroyed, abandoned or made available to other people. The choice is anyone's.

The question of a free store is simply: What would you have?

Street event—birth of haight/funeral for $ now

Pop Art mirrored the social skin. Happenings X-rayed the bones. Street events are social acid heightening consciousness of what is real on the street. To expand eyeball implications until facts are established through action.

The Mexican Day of the Dead is celebrated in cemeteries. Yellow flowers falling petal by petal on graves. In moonlight. Favorite songs of the deceased and everybody gets loaded. Children suck deaths-head candy engraved with their names in icing.

A Digger event. Flowers, mirrors, penny-whistles, girls in costumes of themselves, Hell's Angels, street people, Mime Troupe.

Angels ride up Haight with girls holding Now! signs. Flowers and penny-whistles passed out to everyone.

A chorus on both sides of the street chanting Uhh!—Ahh!—Shh be cool! Mirrors held up to reflect faces of passersby.

The burial procession. Three black-shrouded messengers holding staffs topped with reflective dollar signs. A runner swinging a red lantern. Four pall bearers wearing animal heads carry a black casket filled with blowups of silver dollars. A chorus singing Get Out Of My Life Why Don't You Babe to Chopin's Death March. Members of the procession give out silver dollars and candles.

Now more reality. Someone jumps on a car with the news that two Angels were busted. Crowd, funeral cortege and friends of the Angels fill the street to march on Park Police Station. Cops confront 400 free beings: a growling poet with a lute, animal spirits in black, candle-lit girls singing Silent Night. A collection for bail fills an Angel's helmet. March back to Haight and street dancing.

Street events are rituals of release. Reclaiming of territory (sundown, traffic, public joy) through spirit. Possession. Public NewSense.

Not street-theater, the street is theater. Parades, bank robberies, fires and sonic explosions focus street attention. A crowd is an audience for an event. Release of crowd spirit can accomplish social facts. Riots are a reaction to police theater. Thrown bottles and over-turned cars are responses to a dull, heavy-fisted, mechanical and deathly show. People fill the street to express special public feelings and hold human communion. To ask "What's Happening?"

The alternative to death is a joyous funeral in company with the living.

Who paid for your trip?

Industrialization was a battle with 19th-century ecology to win breakfast at the cost of smog and insanity. Wars against ecology are suicidal. The U.S. standard of living is a bourgeois baby blanket for executives who scream in their sleep. No Pleistocene swamp could match the pestilential horror of modern urban sewage. No children of White Western Progress will escape the dues of peoples forced to haul their raw materials.

But the tools (that's all factories are) remain innocent and the ethics of greed aren't necessary. Computers render the principles of wage-labor obsolete by incorporating them. We are being freed from mechanistic consciousness. We could evacuate the factories, turn them over to androids, clean up our pollution. North Americans could give up self-righteousness to expand their being.

Our conflict is with job-wardens and consumer-keepers of a permissive loony-bin. Property, credit, interest, insurance, installments, profit are stupid concepts. Millions of have-nots and drop-outs in the U.S. are living on an overflow of technologically produced fat. They aren't fighting ecology, they're responding to it. Middle-class living rooms are funeral parlors and only undertakers will stay in them. Our fight is with those who would kill us through dumb work, insane wars, dull money morality.

Give up jobs, so computers can do them! Any important human occupation can be done free. Can it be given away?

Revolutions in Asia, Africa, South America are for humanistic industrialization. The technological resources of North America can be used throughout the world. Gratis. Not a patronizing gift, shared.

Our conflict begins with salaries and prices. The trip has been paid for at an incredible price in death, slavery, psychosis.

An event for the main business district of any U.S. city. Infiltrate the largest corporation office building with life-actors as nymphomaniacal secretaries, clumsy repairmen, berserk executives, sloppy security guards, clerks with animals in their clothes. Low key until the first coffee-break and then pour it on.

Secretaries unbutton their blouses and press shy clerks against the wall. Repairmen drop typewriters and knock over water coolers. Executives charge into private offices claiming their seniority. Guards produce booze bottles and playfully jam elevator doors. Clerks pull out goldfish, rabbits, pigeons, cats on leashes, loose dogs.

At noon 1000 freed beings singing and dancing appear outside to persuade employees to take off for the day. Banners roll down from office windows announcing liberation. Shills in business suits run out of the building, strip and dive in the fountain. Elevators are loaded with incense and a pie fight breaks out in the cafeteria. Theater is fact/action.

Give up jobs. Be with people. Defend against property.

Source: Included in The Digger Papers, August 1968. Reprinted from www.diggers.org, Eric Noble, curator.

9. Excerpt from the Testimony of Abbie Hoffman

The Yippies were the political side of the hippies, landing somewhere between the New Left and the mainstream hipsters. They didn't quite fit in on either side of the divide, but their political antics got more attention than many of the more legitimate activist groups and exhilarated the hippies. When the Yippie leaders were arrested, after their Yip-Out at the Chicago Democratic National Convention of 1968, the trial of the Chicago Seven was the biggest national news story in the hippie community.

This excerpt from the trial testimony of Abbie Hoffman shows not only the Yippies' contempt for the institutions of law and order, but also how hip philosophy appeared when presented side by side with the institutions of mainstream society. Hoffman and Rubin took their testimonies as a prime opportunity to chastise the court and every word was a rejection not only of the authority of the court, but of the American government and the society that created it.

MR. WEINGLASS: Will you please identify yourself for the record?

THE WITNESS: My name is Abbie. I am an orphan of America.

MR. SCHULTZ: Your Honor, may the record show it is the defendant Hoffman who has taken the stand?

THE COURT: Oh, yes. It may so indicate. . . .

MR. WEINGLASS: Where do you reside?

THE WITNESS: I live in Woodstock Nation.

MR. WEINGLASS: Will you tell the Court and jury where it is?

THE WITNESS: Yes. It is a nation of alienated young people. We carry it around with us as a state of mind in the same way as the Sioux Indians carried the Sioux nation around with them. It is a nation dedicated to cooperation versus competition, to the idea that people should have better means of exchange than property or money, that there should be some other basis for human interaction. It is a nation dedicated to—

THE COURT: Just where it is, that is all.

THE WITNESS: It is in my mind and in the minds of my brothers and sisters. It does not consist of property or material but, rather, of ideas and certain values. We believe in a society—

THE COURT: No, we want the place of residence, if he has one, place of doing business, if you have a business. Nothing about philosophy or India, sir. Just where you live, if you have a place to live. Now you said Woodstock. In what state is Woodstock?

THE WITNESS: It is in the state of mind, in the mind of myself and my brothers and sisters. It is a conspiracy. Presently, the nation is held captive, in the penitentiaries of the institutions of a decaying system.

MR. WEINGLASS: Can you tell the Court and jury your present age?

THE WITNESS: My age is 33. I am a child of the 60s.

MR. WEINGLASS: When were you born?

THE WITNESS: Psychologically, 1960.

MR. SCHULTZ: Objection, if the Court please. I move to strike the answer.

MR. WEINGLASS: What is the actual date of your birth?

THE WITNESS: November 30, 1936.

MR. WEINGLASS: Between the date of your birth, November 30, 1936, and May 1, 1960, what if anything occurred in your life?

THE WITNESS: Nothing. I believe it is called an American education.

MR. SCHULTZ: Objection.

THE COURT: I sustain the objection.

THE WITNESS: Huh.

MR. WEINGLASS: Abbie, could you tell the Court and jury—

MR. SCHULTZ: His name isn't Abbie. I object to this informality.

MR. WEINGLASS: Can you tell the Court and jury what is your present occupation?

THE WITNESS: I am a cultural revolutionary. Well, I am really a defendant—full-time.

MR. WEINGLASS: What do you mean by the phrase "cultural revolutionary"?

THE WITNESS: Well, I suppose it is a person who tries to shape and participate in the values, and the mores, the customs and the style of living of new people who eventually become inhabitants of a new nation and a new society through art and poetry, theater, and music.

MR. WEINGLASS: What have you done yourself to participate in that revolution?

THE WITNESS: Well, I have been a rock and roll singer. I am a reporter with the Liberation News Service. I am a poet. I am a film maker. I made a movie called "Yippies Tour Chicago or How I Spent My Summer Vacation." Currently, I am negotiating with United Artists and MGM to do a movie in Hollywood.

I have written an extensive pamphlet on how to live free in the city of New York.

I have written two books, one called Revolution for The Hell of It under the pseudonym Free, and one called, Woodstock Nation.

MR. WEINGLASS: Taking you back to the spring of 1960, approximately May 1, 1960, will you tell the Court and jury where you were?

MR. SCHULTZ: 1960?

THE WITNESS: That's right.

MR. SCHULTZ: Objection.

THE COURT: I sustain the objection.

MR. WEINGLASS: Your Honor, that date has great relevance to the trial. May 1, 1960, was this witness' first public demonstration. I am going to bring him down through Chicago.

THE COURT: Not in my presence, you are not going to bring him down. I sustain the objection to the question.

THE WITNESS: My background has nothing to do with my state of mind?

THE COURT: Will you remain quiet while I am making a ruling? I know you have no respect for me.

MR. KUNSTLER: Your Honor, that is totally unwarranted. I think your remarks call for a motion for a mistrial.

THE COURT: And your motion calls for a denial of the motion. Mr. Weinglass, continue with your examination.

MR. KUNSTLER: You denied my motion? I hadn't even started to argue it.

THE COURT: I don't need any argument on that one. The witness turned his back on me while he was on the witness stand.

THE WITNESS: I was just looking at the pictures of the long hairs up on the wall. . . .

THE COURT: . . . I will let the witness tell about this asserted conversation with Mr. Rubin on the occasion described.

MR. WEINGLASS: What was the conversation at that time?

THE WITNESS: Jerry Rubin told me that he had come to New York to be project director of a peace march in Washington that was going to march to the Pentagon in October, October 21. He said that the peace movement suffered from a certain kind of attitude, mainly that it was based solely on the issue of the Vietnam War. He said that the war in Vietnam was not just an accident but a direct by-product of the kind of system, a capitalist system in the country, and that we had to begin to put forth new kinds of values, especially to young people in the country, to make a kind of society in which a Vietnam war would not be possible.

And he felt that these attitudes and values were present in the hippie movement and many of the techniques, the guerrilla theater techniques that had been used and many of these methods of communication would allow for people to participate and become involved in a new kind of democracy.

I said that the Pentagon was a five-sided evil symbol in most religions and that it might be possible to approach this from a religious point of view. If we got large numbers of people to surround the Pentagon, we could exorcize it of its evil spirits.

So I had agreed at that point to begin working on the exorcism of the Pentagon demonstration.

MR. WEINGLASS: Prior to the date of the demonstration which is October, did you go to the Pentagon?

THE WITNESS: Yes. I went about a week or two before with one of my close brothers, Martin Carey, a poster maker, and we measured the Pentagon, the two of us, to see how many people would fit around it. We only had to do one side because it is just multiplied by five.

We got arrested. It's illegal to measure the Pentagon. I didn't know it up to that point.

When we were arrested they asked us what we were doing. We said it was to measure the Pentagon and we wanted a permit to raise it 300 feet in the air, and they said "How about 10?" So we said "OK."

And they threw us out of the Pentagon and we went back to New York and had a press conference, told them what it was about.

We also introduced a drug called lace, which, when you squirted it at the policemen made them take their clothes off and make love, a very potent drug.

MR. WEINGLASS: Did you mean literally that the building was to rise up 300 feet off the ground?

MR. SCHULTZ: I can't cross-examine about his meaning literally.

THE COURT: I sustain the objection.

MR. SCHULTZ: I would ask Mr. Weinglass please get on with the trial of this case and stop playing around with raising the Pentagon 10 feet or 300 feet off the ground.

MR. WEINGLASS: Your Honor, I am glad to see Mr. Schultz finally concedes that things like levitating the Pentagon building, putting LSD in the water, 10,000 people walking nude on Lake Michigan, and a $200,000 bribe attempt are all playing around. I am willing to concede that fact, that it was all playing around, it was a play idea of this witness, and if he is willing to concede it, we can all go home.

THE COURT: I sustain the objection.

MR. WEINGLASS: Did you intend that the people who surrounded the Pentagon should do anything of a violent nature whatever to cause the building to rise 300 feet in the air and be exercised
of evil spirits?
MR. SCHULTZ: Objection.
THE COURT: I sustain the objection.
MR. WEINGLASS: Could you indicate to the Court and jury
whether or not the Pentagon was, in fact, exercised of its evil spirits?
THE WITNESS: Yes, I believe it was. . . .

Source: Reprinted from University of Missouri–Kansas City Archives.

Life After the Hippies

The hippies fed off the Beats, but who fed off the hippies? While
twenty-somethings were attending the concerts and parties of the hippie
scene, the younger kids, those in the 13–17–year age range, were also
caught up in the flavor of the era. Back in their middle schools and high
schools, they listened to hippie music and donned hip clothing, and
many engaged in junior-league activism and spiritualism. These kids,
just a couple of years behind their older siblings and friends, were the
first group to manifest the effect of the hippie scene in the next decade.

10. Interview with Marcia Sindel

*To many on the East and West coasts, the Midwest is a vast cultureless
wasteland, with the possible exception of Chicago. Despite this prevalent
prejudice, hippie culture flourished in midwestern towns from Omaha to
St. Paul just as it did on the coasts.*

*Marcia Sindel was in her early teens when the Monterey Pop Festival
brought psychedelic rock to the forefront. She was living with her parents
and four brothers in Webster Groves, a small suburb of St. Louis, Missouri.
Though she wasn't in the Haight at the height and didn't visit New York
or California until the 1970s, the counterculture left an indelible mark on
her personality.*

*Sindel's experiences, both in Missouri and later in college and gradu-
ate school at Kansas State University in Lawrence, provide a unique view*

of how the hippie phenomenon left its mark on American life and affected those living outside the major epicenters.

After a divorce, several career changes, and more than a decade spent living with and caring for her aging parents, Sindel became the owner of a small café/bakery, called La Dolce Via (The Sweet Way) in St. Louis City. Her café has an unmistakable touch of the bohemian, from the eclectic décor which includes hand-colored poster art and numerous colorful knick knacks, to the tie-dyed tank top, emblazoned with the company logo, that Sindel chose as a uniform and regularly wears sans brassiere while meeting with customers or baking her delicacies.

In this interview with the author, conducted on January 31, 2009, Sindel talks about growing up in the 1960s and 1970s and the meaning of hippieism to her generation.

MI: When did you first become aware of hippies and what was going on in that counterculture?

MS: I guess seventh grade is when I really started figuring out what was going on. I was into the music, like Cream and the Beatles and the Rolling Stones. In my first 7th-grade picture I had a plaid skirt and a button-down shirt with a tie tack. In my next picture, I had like coveralls or something. I like totally changed.

I moved into my brother's room and painted it yellow with orange curtains so that, when the light came through, the whole room was orange. I had a Jefferson Airplane and a Bob Dylan poster. I had a poster with two rhinoceroses on it, having sex, which said, "Make Love, Not War." I remember when I was on acid it looked like the rhinos were f******. I also had a poster with a black man on it that said, "If Not Now, When?"

I started wearing hippie clothes, like I had this cool shirt that was almost paper material. It was paisley but you could sort of see through it and you could tell I was nude, even though the paisleys covered my nipples. I always wore something purple which was not a big color then and you could never find anything purple in the store. I was known for always wearing purple, like purple socks or a shirt. I had a purple pants suit that was great and I had these knee-high Italian black leather boots, they were killer.

MI: What was it like going to high school in the sixties?

MS: It was different. Our school was really ahead of its time and we had unusual classes. We had a course called American Problems where our teacher would take every issue in America and would present it from the liberal and conservative perspective, then we would have debates. I remember in that class that I wrote a paper on the legalization of marijuana. I also did a paper on the hidden, poor area of Webster Groves. There was a sign when you came into Webster that said "Home of the Beautiful Houses," but there was an area where the houses were almost shacks. This was in North Webster, which was basically the black area of the city. I went and interviewed the people who lived there and they would have to hold the door in place when they opened it because the hinges were so f***** up and the wood was rotten.

The students banded together with the Student Council and got the school to install a smoking lounge. We argued that it would be safer to have the students stay on campus rather than sneaking off and hiding. The whole argument was about honesty and being who you are. When they allowed the smoking lounge, the students respected the rules and they used the ashtrays and kept it clean because it took us a long time to get it.

We also lobbied to have the dress code removed. They had rules that girls had to wear skirts and stocking and/or socks and guys had to wear button-down shirts. We had all of that removed. You could pretty much wear whatever you wanted but you had to have your a** covered and couldn't have any bare midriffs. When Jimi Hendrix died, a s***load of people in the school wore black armbands. I remember that the dress code had just been lifted and the black armbands were questionable. The administration was a little iffy about that.

MI: When did you start experimenting with drugs?

MS: Around ninth grade or so. My brother and his wife turned me on to pot and one night, about that time, I did an acid trip at a friend's house with this friend of mine, Donnie. We sat on the back porch and that was the night I lost my bra. I took it off and never put it back on. I discovered the joys of small breasts and no bra. Donnie said, "Why don't you take it off?" and I did and it was so comfortable.

I had a chemist friend who made acid for me and it was really pure, I didn't have to worry about it being cut with strychnine. I did acid all the time, in high school. The summer before I went to college I got 99 hits of "orange sunshine" from a chemist my brother knew in New Orleans and I finished the whole thing that summer.

When I got to college I still did acid some but slowed down a little bit and got more into just pot. One funny thing of the times; my parents didn't want me to smoke cigarettes but they were okay with me smoking pot. When I smoked a cigarette in their car, I would smoke a joint afterwards to cover the scent. I guess my parents just picked their battles. As long as I got straight *A*s they let me do whatever I wanted.

Every time I go to one of my reunions, I meet another person who came to this party I had at my house. We put acid, woodrose, psilocybin, and mescaline in a big thing of Kool-aid and everybody had to have a glass when they came in the door. A s*** load of people have told me that that was the most memorable night of their high school. My mom sat in the kitchen, not knowing that the kids were tripping, and she just talked to people. She had a ball. She was so great, she would talk about anything. She'd say, "Oh, masturbation is great," and "Oh, nudity is great."

This guy, who called himself "Woodstock," came in drunk. He had right-wing viewpoints and was a real a**hole. He got into this argument and he ended up breaking this glass table that my parents had. For me, that was proof that the alcohol-drinking, right-wing a**holes were out of my life forever.

MI: How did your life change when you went to college?

MS: Well, K.U. was known as the "doper's" school, while the school in Manhattan [Kansas] was known as the drinking school. In Lawrence we had all the great speakers and the great bands coming through, 'cause it was a stop off between San Francisco and New York. I saw Tina Turner and Ike, Crosby Stills and Nash, the Youngbloods, and the Young Rascals. We got all this new and exciting stuff in the classes too, like we had an entire class on genealogy.

MI: Were you married while you were in college?

MS: Greg lived in a rehabbed fraternity house and I worked at a bar down the street. When I first met him he was on academic probation and he was basically flunking out of school; he was a philosophy major [laughs]. Well we broke up, and he was really upset and did really bad that semester. I met him again one day and he was telling me that he hadn't met anyone he was really comfortable with. He had just come back from this trip to New Orleans with this woman and he had terrible sex. I made the suggestion that we become f*** buddies and wouldn't put anything on it. We would just hang out together and have sex. From then on it was doom. We had great sex. There was no way we weren't gonna really get involved. We really liked each other.

That summer we moved in together with two of our best friends into this old house. The guys painted "love" in big block letters up the stairway. We painted one of the bathrooms rainbow and one was purple. My friend Jeannie and I made all the curtains for the house. We had this humidor that we used for all of our pot stuff. We had a TV, but we really didn't do TV that much. We listened to a lot of music and we had a stereo system through the whole house.

I had already had an abortion and I got pregnant in 1974, at least I thought I was. I told Greg that I wasn't going to have another abortion and we decided to get married. Then like, a week before the wedding, I started my period, so I said, "Do you want to do it anyway?" and he said "yeah," so we did it.

We had our wedding back in Webster at the Monday Club. There was no food and there were like 40 people. We had this 1940s band, which I got 'cause they knew how to play my parents' favorite song, "Stardust."

I had this black preacher and everyone thought that I did it on purpose, 'cause that was totally "me" to force the racial issue, but it was just a fluke. I asked another preacher but he wasn't available and called in a friend of his from Saint Louis and the guy just turned out to be black. It was just perfect for my personality even though I hadn't planned it.

We each walked out with both parents and, before we came out, the preacher asked people to tell what they thought of our union and we listened from behind the scene. It was all good, what they said, nobody was honest (laughs). Then we came out and we did the ceremony and read our vows, which we wrote together.

I remember we had this couple from Lawrence there and they were Sufis so everyone did some Sufi dancing and chanting after the ceremony. Greg and all the men, his father and my father, were on their knees doing one chant and all the women danced around them and chanted something else. It was really bizarre seeing Greg and his dad on their knees. I had my old pediatrician there and she was dancing and chanting with us; everybody participated.

My parents went and stayed with my brother and his wife and we took their bedroom for our wedding night. The next day we all had to drive back to school.

MI: When did you have your first child?

MS: I had my first child during my last year at college. One of my classes was an independent study course and I did this whole project on the process of being pregnant, like I took pictures every week to show how my body changed.

I remember I had this class called "Altered States of Consciousness," and we studied the chemical effects, on the brain, of different drugs, yoga, meditation, and sensory deprivation. My paper for that class was on masturbation and the teacher loved it. The next year, because of that paper, I was the T.A. My teacher, whose name was Mike, brought me a silver cup when my child was born. Mike was an openly gay teacher and that was really different at the time. By and large it wasn't a big deal and everyone was really accepting of it. I remember that my paper was very erotically written and he told me, "That's the closest I've come to being turned on by anything about a woman in years."

When my daughter was born, I would bring her to class and nurse her in the classroom. The first class I did it in was a human sexuality class and everyone, at first, seemed appalled. I said, "These are my milk bottles, if you want to look at them as t*** and get turned on, that's your problem." By the end of the class, people would sit right next to me and play with my daughter while I was nursing. The year after that, the school started a day care.

MI: What did the hippie movement mean to you at the time?

MS: The hippie movement pushed me towards self-reliance. My definition of a hippie was someone who was trying to live off the earth. We belonged to a co-op and had a garden in the back yard. We cooked for ourselves and made bread and just, lived simply.

It was also about not getting pushed into a sexual identity. We all wore overalls and there was no dressing up or wearing make-up.

All the women in my group stopped wearing deodorant and shaving their legs and armpits. There was a woman on campus who worked for a lawn and garden place and the guys who worked there would take off their shirts when they were working in the summer and so she took off hers too. She got arrested like three times but she kept doing it.

There was a focus about accepting everybody and trying to get to know people until you figured them out and accepted them. In the fifties it seemed like everyone was interested in what was best for society and there wasn't a lot of individuality. The beginning of what they called the "me era" was that you have to know what you feel and what you want in order to have those feelings and desires considered. Everyone was trying to figure themselves out so they knew what they were doing in life. It was a big era of self-examination and self-critique but it got flummoxed into this thing of "It's a free country and I can do whatever I want." What I took away from it was that what I feel and what I think matters.

MI: What elements of that hippie message are still with you today?

MS: I think the biggest thing that the hippie movement did for me is probably evident in my marriage. All this stuff went on between us and we're still friends. That is all part of the '60s and '70s, because we were figuring out who we were. It taught me to look at the whole process and realize that the divorce wasn't his fault and it wasn't mine and there was no reason to make it a deal breaker. That is the biggest thing I took away from that time: the ability to look at a painful situation for what it is and face it.

I believe that there is a certain harmony to my life and my relationships that came from that whole time where I learned to look beyond myself and my feelings and also beyond society and everything else and just look at the situation, the way it is, and learn to accept it. That's what I think of when I think of the era—I think of people being able to look at each other as who they are and be okay with it. To be more accepting of one another.

The drugs were just a vehicle for breaking down the barriers. We had a rule where, whenever we got together we hugged and whenever we separated we hugged. I said, "Just hug 'cause, from the moment you hug you've broken a barrier and everything has changed." Do whatever it takes to break down the barrier that is keeping you from knowing a person and then you move on.

Annotated Bibliography

Books

Allyn, David Smith. *Make Love Not War: The Sexual Revolution, an Unfettered History.* New York: Little, Brown, 2000.

Allyn ranged far and wide to find information for his history of the sexual revolution, speaking to feminist organizers, porn stars, and manufacturers of birth control products. Allyn combines a historical analysis with interviews, from people on either side of various debates, to discover how the changes that America experienced during the sexual revolution manifested in the lives of the American people. Allyn's discussion of feminism and sex roles in the 1960s is especially enlightening for anyone researching hippies as he deftly compares and contrasts the sex roles that were the hippies' ideal, with the reality they helped to create.

Altman, Robert. *The Sixties.* Santa Monica, CA: Santa Monica Press, 2007.

Photographer Robert Altman provided the pictures and much of the commentary for this book, which is an excellent introduction to the hippie era. Altman's photographs portray hippie leaders, musical legends, and the hippies who followed them with clarity and a sensitive eye. Framing his pictures, Altman provides interesting first-hand commentary, made more fascinating as he was a witness to the development of the psychedelic music scene from its roots.

Beard, Rick. *Greenwich Village: Culture and Counterculture.* New Brunswick, NJ: Rutgers University Press, 1993.

A comprehensive picture of Greenwich Village that includes both the Beat Generation and the hippie era and shows how the decline of one culture leads to the next. Includes profiles and histories of some of the neighborhood's notable hippie-era residents as well as a modern perspective on the development of Greenwich after the sixties.

Booth, Martin. *Cannabis: A History.* New York: Macmillan, 2005.

In this fascinating history of *Cannabis sativa*, better known as marijuana, Booth takes readers from the first-known use of the plant through its prohibition and rehabilitation as a medical aid. Booth investigates controversial topics, like government propaganda programs designed to discourage marijuana use, to the drug's deification in cults and religious groups around the world. Booth also looks at the marijuana issue from a strictly economic viewpoint, examining the cost of prohibition, the potential costs and benefits of legalization, and the use of the drug in the underground economy. Booth's book is particularly useful for its exploration of marijuana use in the 1960s, when it was the most popular hippie drug next to LSD.

Cavan, Sherri. *Hippies of the Haight.* St. Louis, MO: New Critics Press, 1972.

Dr. Cavan, a sociologist at San Francisco State University, produced this informative and enjoyable study of hippie culture while the hippies were moving in, setting up shop, and moving out of her own neighborhood: the famous Haight Ashbury. While Cavan's language and research methods may seem dated by modern standards, hers is the only "street-level" view of hippie culture and one of the most valuable sources on the transformation of the Haight Ashbury neighborhood from progressive blue-collar enclave to cultural capital of the West Coast hippie scene.

Charters, Ann. *The Portable Sixties Reader.* New York: Penguin Classics, 2003.

Charters's excellent book collects hundreds of short articles and essays, interspersed with short fiction and poetry, to help illustrate the diversity of a turbulent period. Charters organizes her material into themed chapters, including counterculture, drugs, and the anti-Vietnam movement. Charters's collection is enjoyable and easy to read, making it suitable for those preparing scholarly works or simply looking to experience some examples of the intellectual flavor of the decade.

Cohen, Allen. *The San Francisco Oracle: Facsimile Edition.* Berkeley, CA: Regent Press, 1990.

The complete collection of photos, articles, and advertisements originally published in the *San Francisco Oracle* from September 3, 1966, to February 1968. This is the premier alternative press newspaper, in terms of style, production value, and content, and the articles contained within provide an invaluable view of hippie life and culture. The photos and advertisements found in the *Oracle* are a treasure for historians and sixties aficionados and provide a unique view into the culture of Haight Ashbury at the heights of the hippie era.

DeGroot, Gerard. *The Sixties Unplugged: A Kaleidoscopic History of a Disorderly Decade*. New York: Macmillan, 2008.

> DeGroot, a history professor at the University of St. Andrews, Scotland, created a penetrating and insightful look at the sixties in the United States and abroad. Written in short snippets, each focusing on an important event and/ or figure, DeGroot describes Malcolm X, the end of colonialism in Africa, the rise of the Students for a Democratic Society (SDS), and numerous other aspects of sixties culture and lifestyle. Valuable as an introduction to the decade and for DeGroot's penetrating analysis and commentary, examining both the origins and the fate of sixties culture and counterculture.

Echols, Alice. *Shaky Ground: The 60s and Its Aftershocks*. New York: Columbia University Press, 2002.

> Echols, a veteran writer on feminist issues and pop culture, creates an unusual and unique history of the 1960s with an eye toward the theme of cultural change and revolution at the grassroots level. Through interviews with well-known icons of the era and detailed examinations of historical developments, Echols creates a thesis that the social changes that were initiated in the 1960s continued well into the 1970s and continue to leave an imprint on American culture. Echols's work is particularly valuable for her discussion of women in the 1960s and changing attitudes about gender and roles in society.

Farber, David. *Chicago '68*. Chicago: University of Chicago Press, 1994.

> Historian David Farber creates an exhaustive investigation of the Chicago 1968 Democratic National Convention protests from their origins to the resulting trial of the Chicago Seven in 1969. Useful both as a history of the Yippies and hippie activism and as a look at how the Chicago Seven trial revealed aspects of the American legal and justice system. Farber also used his analysis to delve into the history of the Black Panther Party and member Bobby Seale, the eighth member of those arrested for their participation in the 1968 Chicago riots. Farber's investigation of the trial itself is especially illuminating as it avoids the dogma of other, less comprehensive accounts, and presents the facts with a fair eye toward the motivations of both sides.

Friedlander, Paul. *Rock and Roll: A Social History*. New York: Westview Press, 1996.

> Friedlander provides an excellent source of information about the history and development of the American rock scene. Among other topics, Friedlander covers the British Invasion and the dawn and decline of psychedelic rock as well as providing biographical sketches of some of the era's biggest talents. Particularly insightful is Friedlander's analysis about the transformation of sixties rock into seventies singer/songwriters, a musical analog for the cultural changes on a grander scale.

Gair, Christopher. *The American Counterculture*. Edinburgh: University of Edinburgh Press, 2007.

Gair, a lecturer in American literature, lends a discerning eye to the development and popularization of the American counterculture, from the Beat Generation and the hippies to more recent trends. Gair looks especially at how the popular media and entertainment media learned to cater to the counterculture as consumers and how this affected the development of counterculture values and beliefs. Gair's analysis is deeply detailed and provides information on the philosophical grounding that underlies the development of counterculture movements, in addition to looking at the more lighthearted aspects of counterculture behavior.

Grunenberg, Christoph, and Jonathan Harris. *Summer of Love: Psychedelic Art, Social Crisis and Counterculture in the 1960s.* Liverpool: Liverpool University Press, 2005.

Editors Grunenberg and Harris provide a look at the Summer of Love and 1960s counterculture through the art of the era. Filled with paintings, sculpture, and graphic art from the period, this history is as much a visual exploration as it is a sensitive and intelligent view of the period from a modern perspective. The editors invite essays from figures representing many different perspectives on 1960s culture and society. Particularly interesting is the discussion of fashion and architecture of the 1960s and how it related to the cultural changes that the nation was experiencing.

Gurvis, Sandra. *Where Have All the Flower Children Gone?* Jackson: University Press of Mississippi, 2006.

Gurvis's book, told through the stories of aging hippies and 1960s activists, provides an interesting first hand account of the era removed by several decades from the turbulent drama of the sixties. Gurvis also delves into the student protest movement, examining the history of, among others, members of the Students for a Democratic Society (SDS) and the Student Nonviolent Coordinating Committee (SNCC). Gurvis concludes her investigation by looking at how hippies of the 1960s maintained their ideals, or lost them, as they transitioned to the 21st century.

Hicks, Michael. *Sixties Rock: Garage, Psychedelic, and Other Satisfactions.* Champaign: University of Illinois Press, 2000.

Taking information from the entire history of rock music and its predecessors, Hicks examines, specifically, the subgenres of "garage rock" and "psychedelic rock," looking at how the genres emerged and the effect they had on the music scene at large. Hicks's investigation of the sixties music scene in Haight-Ashbury is especially useful, speaking about how the bands got started, the advent of psychedelic lighting and underground concerts, and the push into the mainstream with concerts like the Monterey Pop Festival.

Lee, Martin A., and Bruce Shlain. *Acid Dreams: The Complete Social History of LSD: The CIA, the Sixties and Beyond.* New York: Grove Press, 1992.

Lee and Shlain investigate sixties culture through one of its most important facets, the development and popularization of LSD. Most interesting is the book's investigation of the relationship between LSD and American law and the use of LSD as a psychiatric aid. Lee and Shlain also provide interesting biographical accounts of some of the hippie era's most renowned figures, like Timothy Leary and Ken Kesey, though their involvement with acid cults.

Leland, John. *Hip: The History*. New York: Harper Collins, 2004.

Leland's investigation of the idea of "hip" provides not only an interesting view of how the word was co-opted by hippie society to stand for their own worldview, but also serves as an interesting investigation of race relations and the development of counterculture and language in America. Leland's easily accessible prose invites readers to explore various facets of underground America from 1940s jazz clubs to the discos of the 1970s. Leland extends the meaning of hip to the modern era, examining what persons and phenomena qualify as hip in the modern world.

Lytle, Mark H. *America's Uncivil Wars: The Sixties Era from Elvis to the Fall of Richard Nixon*. New York: Oxford University Press, 2006.

Historian Lytle takes a broad look at a complicated decade attempting to make sense of the intricately interwoven threads that contributed to the politics and cultural changes of the decade. The book is extremely valuable for its discussion of the various predisposing factors that led America into the 1960s, such as McCarthyism and the effects of World War II. Lytle also reaches beyond the sixties to create a cogent view of the next decade as a reflection of the sixties, the counterculture, and the rapidly changing nature of American culture.

McFarlane, Scott. *The Hippie Narrative: A Literary Perspective on the Counterculture*. Jefferson, NC: McFarland Publications, 2007.

In this intelligent history, McFarlane looks at the literature from the 1950s to the 1970s and uses essays, published books, manifestos, and poetry to create a picture of the counterculture from a variety of perspectives. Among the more interesting points of McFarlane's analysis is his discussion of the ideological distinctions between the Beats and the hippies and how this manifested in the writing and other cultural products of both groups. McFarlane's analysis of the works of early Beat writers also helps to prepare the stage for the hippie phenomenon and provide valuable insights as to where the hippies derived their sense of aesthetics and philosophy.

Miller, Timothy. *The Hippies and American Values*. Knoxville: University of Tennessee Press, 1991.

In preparing this book, Miller relied heavily on articles published in the alternative press. Using quotes and ideas taken from newspapers like the *Berkeley Barb* and the *San Francisco Oracle*, Miller provides a clear and captivating look at hippie philosophy, values, and ethnics. Miller's fascinating and insightful discussion of hippie approaches to community and sexuality are among the book's high points, as the author manages to find and illustrate the factors that set the hippies apart from their parents and, ultimately, their children.

Morgan, Bill. *The Beat Generation in San Francisco: A Literary Tour.* San Francisco: City Lights Books, 2003.

> Morgan provides a deep exposition of how Beat culture developed and spread in San Francisco, from the cafés of North Beach to the early Haight neighborhood, before the arrival of the hippies. Morgan also covers the relationship between Beats on the West and East coasts as he weaves a detailed view of the San Francisco Beat scene. Also valuable as a source of knowledge about the relationship between the hippies and the Beats and about the lives of figures important to both groups, like Allen Ginsberg, Lawrence Ferlinghetti, and Ken Kesey.

Perry, Charles. *The Haight-Ashbury: A History.* New York: Wenner Publishers, 2005.

> Perry's history of the Haight-Ashbury neighborhood and the hippie scene that developed there is interesting and informative, as Perry not only speaks about the development of the neighborhood, but also provides insight into the culture that existed there. Among other subjects, Perry focuses heavily on the music scene in the Haight and its manifestation through promoters like Chet Helms and Bill Graham. Another interesting facet to Perry's analysis is the examination of movement between and among counterculture neighborhoods in San Francisco and how the residents, and the city's government, responded to the development of one of the nation's largest counterculture communities.

Torgoff, Martin. *Can't Find My Way Home: America in the Great Stoned Age.* New York: Simon and Schuster, 2004.

> Historian and documentarian Torgoff investigates the development and consequences of drug culture in America, covering 1950s and 1960s counterculture, government prohibition, and changing attitudes about drug use among the American populace. Torgoff's history is told partially though investigative journalism and partially through first-person accounts of drug culture from the 1940s through the 1990s. As he develops his central arguments, Torgoff neither celebrates nor condemns recreational drug use, but prefers to provide a middle-ground perspective, looking at the negative and positive aspects to drugs in America. Torgoff's discussions of 1960s counterculture are particularly enlightening as they examine the 1960s from a perspective rooted in the advent and popularization of drug culture.

Turner, Fred. *From Counterculture to Cyberculture.* Chicago: University of Chicago Press, 2006.

> Turner provides a fascinating account of the ways in which the American counterculture, especially the hippies and other groups active in the 1960s, continue to leave their mark on American society. Through his examinations of the digital culture of the 21st century, Turner looks at cultural developments like Stewart Brand's Whole Earth Catalog as the forerunners of a new, digital age. Turner also looks at how the phenomenon of counterculture itself has changed and adapted to the new modes of expression and organization offered by the digital environment.

Young, Nigel. *An Infantile Disorder?: The Crisis and Decline of the New Left*. New York: Routledge, 1977.

Though a somewhat dated analysis, Young's history of the New Left, including in-depth investigations of the Students for a Democratic Society, the Students Nonviolent Coordinating Committee, and the League for Industrial Democracy, still stands as an authoritative investigation of the liberalist movement of the 1960s and 1970s. Young examines the emergence of the New Left and its inspirations, both philosophical and political, and then examines the development of the most important groups and their participation in protests, demonstrations, and other political actions. Young also takes time to look at terrorism and radical splinter groups that emerged and diverged from the New Left leaders.

Zimmerman, Nadya. *Counterculture Kaleidoscope: Musical and Cultural Perspectives on Late Sixties San Francisco*. Ann Arbor: University of Michigan Press, 2008.

Zimmerman provides an interesting, scholarly look at the culture of late-sixties San Francisco, largely through the development of the city's music scene. The most interesting facet of Zimmerman's work is her view that the counterculture of the hippies was not a committed social movement but was, rather, a collection of young people who embraced a wide variety of worldviews.

Film and Documentary

Davis, David (producer, writer, director) and Stephen Talbot (writer, producer). *The Sixties: The Years That Shaped the Generation*. Documentary. PBS Studios, 2005.

This documentary investigates the sixties through the major issues of the time including the civil rights struggle, the Vietnam conflict, and the rise of the American counterculture. Interviews with important counterculture figures like Peter Coyote and Arlo Guthrie are supplemented by archival interviews and footage of sixties events in the United States and around the world. An invaluable introduction to the sixties bolstered by a treasure trove of rare footage and insightful commentary.

Dolgin, Gail (Writer, director, producer) and Vicente Franco (writer, director, producer). *American Experience: Summer of Love*. Documentary. PBS Studios, 2007.

This documentary focuses, specifically, on the culture of the Haight-Ashbury and San Francisco in the late 1960s, especially the period surrounding the summer of 1967. Interviews with important hippie era figures are interspersed with footage from San Francisco showing the street scene at the height of the Bay Area hippie scene. In this both entertaining and informative work, Dolgin and Franco have created an excellent primer for anyone interested in American history, hippie culture, or San Francisco's turbulent past.

Multimedia

Cohen, Allan. *The San Francisco Oracle: A Complete Digital Recreation of the Legendary Psychedelic Underground Newspaper Originally Published in the Haight Ashbury During the Summer of Love.* CD ROM. Berkeley, CA: Regent Press, 2006.

> This CD-ROM contains the entire collection of the *San Francisco Oracle* and is the electronic version of the book listed above and the source of several original articles and images reprinted in this volume.

Web Resources

Cockrell, Kathy. "Listening for the Not-So-Faint Echo of the '60s." UC Berkeley News, Berkeleyan, May 3, 2006. www.berkeley.edu/news/berkeleyan/2006/05/03_communes.shtml.

> Article from the Public Affairs section of the UC Berkeley News Online discussing scholarly explorations of communes and communards from a modern sociological perspective. Particularly interesting is the discussion about which elements of hippie culture in general modern communards chose to retain and how hippie ideals have changed in the decades since the 1960s.

Erowid: Documenting the Complex Relationship Between Humans and Psychoactives. "Erowid Vault." EROWID, 2009. www.erowid.com.

> This website, created by a group called Erowid, contains a variety of articles, reprinted documents and encyclopedic entries concerning the history, legal status, and use of psychoactive substances. Useful for its information about the legal history of hallucinogens and marijuana in the United States and for their collection of interesting articles about legalization of substances.

The Farm Official Website. "Lifestyle." The Farm, Summertown, Tennessee, 2007. www.thefarm.org.

> A collection of information about The Farm commune in Summertown, Tennessee, one of the longest lasting communes in the United States. Useful as a resource for exploring how hippie ideals translated into lifestyle choices and how the hippies of the 1960s have shifted their focus in the 21st century. Also interesting are sections providing information about sustainable agriculture and community involvement.

Good, Thomas, ed. "Next Left Notes." Next Left Notes, 2009. www.antiauthoritarian.net/NLN/.

> Next Left Notes is a continuation of the original "New Left Notes" created by the Students for the Democratic Society as a free newsletter to disseminate information about the activities and goals of the student activist movement. The official website also contains information on the history of the New Left, the Students for a Democratic Society, and other student movements. Useful as a source of information about the transformation of hippie culture.

Hip Inc. "Hippieland." www.hippy.com.

> Hip Media provides articles, an online dictionary, and a set of useful links to everything hippie oriented. Of particular interest is the site's collection of "topics," ranging from vegetarianism to drugs, which collect articles, historical information, and a variety of other information about how the hippies approached various issues.

The History Channel. "Hippies—1968." A&E Television Networks, 2008. www.history.com/states.do?action=state&state=Hippies&parentId=1968.

> An excellent presentation on hippies and hippie music from the History Channel, featuring articles, videos, and commentary. Also includes information about the civil rights movement and the anti-Vietnam movement of the 1960s. Of particular interest are the original performances from some of the era's most notable bands and musicians. A good source of basic information with links and references to materials useful for more in-depth study.

Noble, Eric. "The Diggers Archives." www.diggers.org.

> Site architect Eric Noble's collection of artifacts, articles, and other resources related to both the San Francisco Diggers and the seventeenth-century English society by the same name. Noble provides both a wealth of original documents and articles by and about members of the Diggers, giving an invaluable look at how the group functioned in San Francisco hippie culture.

University Library Special Collections Digital Center. "The Psychedelic 60s: Literary Tradition and Social Change." University of Virginia, 2008. www2.lib.virginia.edu/exhibits/sixties/index.html.

> The University of Virginia's collection of articles and digitized material from the sixties is an invaluable resource. Original speeches, articles, and hippie writings are interspersed with commentary examining the 1960s from a modern viewpoint. The site also contains information on the student protest movement and the Beat movement, with emphasis on how the Beats and student activists interacted with the hippies and youth of the 1960s.

Index

About the Author

MICAH L. ISSITT is a freelance writer living and working in Philadelphia, Pennsylvania. He has contributed his work to newspapers, magazines, and academic publications. Mr. Issitt specializes in animal behavior/ethnology, history, ethnography and the dynamics of social systems.